# Improv to Improve Your Leadership Team

# Improv to Improve Your Leadership Team

## Tear Down Walls and Build Bridges

Candy Campbell

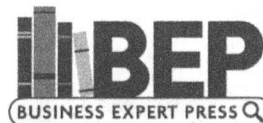

**BEP**

BUSINESS EXPERT PRESS

*Leader in applied, concise business books*

First published in 2023 by
Business Expert Press, LLC
222 East 46th Street, New York, NY 10017
www.businessexpertpress.com

ISBN-13: 978-1-63742-428-5 (paperback)
ISBN-13: 978-1-63742-429-2 (e-book)

Business Expert Press Human Resource Management and Organizational Behavior Collection

First edition: 2023

10 9 8 7 6 5 4 3 2 1

*To all those leaders who desire to leave this world*
*a better place than they found it.*

# Description

**You're a leader with a problem.** There's a fungus-like growth in your organizational culture you can no longer ignore. It starts slowly with a few people feeling maligned and/or excluded, spreads resentment, leads to disengagement, and finally…resignations.

What a nightmare!

**But WAIT!** You have stumbled onto the exact solution you need!

With this book, you can QUICKLY discover how to use the principles of applied improvisational exercises from the arts to help teams effectively connect and communicate, creatively problem-solve, increase workplace safety and employee retention, and guarantee client and stakeholder satisfaction. It's all contained here.

## Keywords

improv; leader; leadership; servant leadership; cultural transformation; transformational leadership; teamwork; team building; applied improvisational exercises; AIEs; applied improv; improv for business; employee engagement; employee retention; joy at work; icebreakers; diversity; equity; inclusion; inclusivity; sense of belonging; workplace culture; employee problems; workplace issues; bullying; conflict resolution

# Contents

# Testimonials

*"Dr. Campbell has done something truly remarkable. By combining the fun and creativity of improv with documented, empirical research, she has written a user's manual for building a cohesive, energized, and effective team. Leaders, take note: when you follow Campbell's blueprint, your team will feel more valued, more respected, and more engaged."*—**Bill Stainton, CSP, CPAE, 29-time Emmy Winner, Hall of Fame Innovation Speaker**

*"Candy Campbell is an extraordinary person and she has written an extraordinary book. I highly recommend you read it, then re-read it and share it with people in your network who want to grow as leaders!"*—**Dr. Willie Jolley, Hall of Fame Speaker, Syndicated Radio Show Host and Best-Selling Author**, *A Setback Is a Setup for a Comeback* **and** *An Attitude of Excellence!*

*"Improv to Improve reminds leaders, at all levels, of the need to constantly reassess their organizational culture, their educational and training initiatives, and their own leadership responses. With her friendly approach, Candy makes learning about leadership approachable and relevant."*—**Commander Mary C. Kelly, author**, *The Five Minute Leadership Guide*

*"The labor market is tight and will remain so for years due to the demographics of the aging population and low immigration. The companies that survive—and thrive—will be those that focus on employee retention, recruitment, and productivity. Dr. Campbell's new book provides a valuable instrument for the business manager's toolbox.*

*The focus of the book is always on improving business teams' performance through better cooperation and communication. The fun side of improv—while well described—takes a backseat to the goal of improving productivity. And research on worker performance clearly demonstrates that employee engagement and productivity connects to employee retention."*—**Dr. Bill Conerly, PhD, business economist**, *Forbes* **senior contributor, Duke University**

*"All leadership happens on a stage, from colleagues who are fellow actors to an audience of customers and shareholders. Thankfully, Dr. Candy Campbell has written the definitive script on how embracing the principle of Improv will improve our leadership teams. It's more than a book, it is complete with detailed exercises in every chapter. It's more than dialogue and a set, she has seamlessly shown us how to engage our colleagues rather than direct them, how to listen to create rather than respond and how to know when to step to center stage or set up a colleague to steal the show!* Improv to Improve Your Leadership Team *is a must read and a must do!*

*This is the most complete text I have reviewed that deals with improv or extemporaneous strategies to develop a team."*—**Barry Banther, author of** ***A Leader's Gift—How to Earn the Right to be Followed***; **Past Chair of the National Speaker's Association, Hall of Fame Speaker, and nationally recognized business leadership adviser**

*"If you're looking for specific techniques to help your team 'open up,' communicate more candidly, and become more connected, check out this book. Dr. Candy Campbell's step-by-step instructions will help you facilitate breakthrough conversations with your team."*—**Liz Weber, President, Weber Business Services, LLC**

*"As a seasoned speaker and speech coach, I have experienced decades of Candy Campbell presentations and performances. Her dedication to healthcare professionals has expanded to the world of business. Her book* Improv to Improve Your Leadership Team *is designed to help leaders committed to find new and better techniques to communicate. Chocked full of examples that will enrich both your business and your personal life."*—**Patricia Fripp, CSP, CPAE, Past President National Speakers Association**

*"Dr. Candy Campbell's new book successfully attacks an age-old problem … human nature. What an awesome resource for cultural transformation. Study the content and apply the exercises and you'll have a formula for success. I'm thinking the book should have been titled, Effectiveness through Fun!"*—**Ed Rigsbee, CSP, CAE, President Rigsbee Research, Executive Director Cigar PEG Philanthropy through Fun, Co-Founder Association and Society Speakers Community, author of *The Art of Partnering;***

*Developing Strategic Alliances; PartnerShift; Member ROI-the Missing Link for Explosive Growth*

*"There are many leadership books available to each of us. Many with new slogans and acronyms. Many with new tactics. But here is the truth: New slogans and acronyms and new tactics do not create better leaders; they do not change culture; they do not lead to betterment.*

*Leadership is about relationships. First with oneself and secondly with those we lead and serve. And these relationships must be built on a solid foundation of authenticity and vulnerability and caring (each leading to trust).*

*Dr. Candy Campbell, in her new book* Improv to Improve Your Leadership Team, *leverages her many years in healthcare, in business, and on stage to provide a practical resource for each of us to look in the mirror, to be present with those we are blessed to lead and serve, to connect and engage, to focus on them, and to become better leaders as we also foster a new culture built on a foundation of trust and care. And she does so following the evidence (the science) including the importance of gratitude and fun(and so much more) in learning and growing.*

*From* Improv to Improve Your Leadership Team *you will walk away with experiences (improv exercises) to implement with your team which will have you each learning, growing, improving … and laughing. You will look in the mirror (I know I did) and see opportunities to be better (and you will want to be better). And now you will know the how (along with why) and be ready to move into action (improv action) today.*

*Thank you, Dr. Campbell, for sharing such practical and essential wisdom in such a creative way which positions us all to be better for self and others."*
—**Tom Dahlborg, President and CEO, Dahlborg HealthCARING Leadership Group, LLC**

*"Candy Campbell did a masterful job with her book* Improv to Improve Your Leadership Team. *In this time of the great resignation, Candy focuses on the crucial element of workplace culture—communication.*

*This book is a must-read for leaders looking to up their communication game in a fun, compelling, and effective way. You'll find many activities that you can easily implement with your team and see immediate results. As long as you are willing to step out of your comfort zone, try something different, and don't take yourself so seriously, you and your team will benefit from bringing in a little improv to improve your company culture. Thanks so much, Candy, for writing this book and introducing this content at a time when it is so desperately needed."*—**Lisa Ryan, CSP, Chief Appreciation Strategist at Grategy**

*"Candy Campbell clearly knows her stuff! She does an outstanding job of showing the reader how improv can play a crucial role in our work. It isn't just a technique for stage, it is an action for life!"*—**Laurie Guest, CSP, CPAE, Author and Hall of Fame Speaker**

*"Creativity and innovation are vital to create change and positive transformations in today's business enterprise. In* Improv to Improve your Leadership Team, *Dr. Candy Campbell has created a playbook for leaders to activate creativity, innovation, and an improvisational leadership style. She shares principles, practices, tips, and resources that will reframe and transform the way you approach your everyday leadership responsibilities. Read her book, practice the techniques, and be surprised about the differences in culture you can create with an improvisational mind set."*—**Daniel J. Pesut, PhD, RN, FAAN, Emeritus Professor, and Emeritus Chair in Nursing Leadership, University of Minnesota School of Nursing**

*"Who knew that the skills needed to be a master of comedy and improv could be translated into leadership skills that can help managers in the workplace? Dr. Candy Campbell knew.*

*In her new book,* Improv to Improve Your Leadership Team: Tear Down Walls and Build Bridges, *Candy not only leads you through the development of such skills as adaptability, facilitation, and building empathy, she also gives you real-life examples of how improv skills can heighten your level of learning in all these areas. The fact that she has so much experience in the improv, entertainment, and management fields just adds to the credibility with which she speaks and writes.*

*If you are searching for a leadership resource that has a truly unique view of how to motivate and inspire your leadership team, this is the book for you.*

Improv to Improve Your Leadership Team *can be your guide to increased productivity, higher employee retention, and greater customer satisfaction."*
**—Mark Levin, CAE CSP, President B.A.I., Inc., Past President, National Speakers Association-DC**

*"In an age when we have never been more distracted, a leader's ability to be fully present is critical. It is the source of their capacity to listen, to include all voices, to be creative, and to adapt rapidly to change.* Improv to Improve Your Leadership Team *offers a practical and fun way to achieve this elusive skill. Dr. Campbell enlightens us with the power of improv to shorten the learning curve for building dynamic and innovative teams. It is jam-packed with exercises that help teams learn pivotal leadership skills in a unique way. What's more in a time when workplace stress has never been higher this book will help bring fun and laughter back into your team."*—**Dr. Irvine Nugent, CSP, Emotional Intelligence expert, author of *Leadership Lessons From the Pub***

*"After 55 years in the business world, I thought I knew all I needed to know about leadership. Dr. Campbell just taught me there is so much I still need to learn! Easy and enjoyable read. Great stories, great examples, and the book easily becomes a workbook for leadership training!"*—**Chuck Hooper, Business Intelligence consultant and start-up coach**

*"In her book,* Improv to Improve Your Leadership Team: Tear Down Walls and Build Bridges, *Dr. Candy Campbell offers fresh, compelling, and well-researched insights into the amazing world of leadership. Its instant read-ability and powerfully adaptable teambuilding practices make this book a real winner for anyone in any industry. Introducing the principles of applied improvisational exercises into your organization offers a fun, exciting, and encouraging way to build a psychologically safe culture, where employees not only want to, but look forward to coming to work each day.*

*After leading large teams numbering in the hundreds and studying and teaching leadership for well over two decades, I have now discovered a book that truly brings new, innovative ways of thinking to help successfully grow my team, our organization, and me personally as a leader. This book is a definite must read for all leaders and it is sure to help improve interpersonal communications, problem-solving skills, team efficiencies, employee and customer happiness and satisfaction, company culture, employee retention rates, and the organizations bottom-line."*—**J.R. Glascock, COSS, RSO, President of LeadershipTopix.com, Director of Corporate QHSE, Lane Construction Corporation**

*"This book is well organized and clearly explains the benefits of having a structured improv workshop led by an experienced trainer. Corporations that embrace improv workshops have much to gain. Employees will learn better ways to communicate with each other especially when it comes to listening and thinking of new solutions to problems.*

*The step-by-step exercises described in this book are easy to follow. A team of new employees, as well as veterans, can all sharpen their thinking skills and surprise themselves and others with the outcomes of the improv workshops.*

*The twelve Improv Principles are shared at the beginning of this book and explained in the chapters that follow. Many of these principles are good practices to follow to improve active listening skills with our partners, spouses, children, family, and co-workers."*—**Rosemarie Rossetti, PhD, CEO and Founder, Rossetti Enterprises LLC. Accessible Design, Universal Design, Aging in Place, Disability Inclusion and Embracing Change Expert**

*"Yes! Fun, comedy, and experimentation to solve serious leadership challenges —it's a delicious recipe for building a culture of excellence. This book elegantly connects the liberating and energizing concepts of Improv to those situations that leaders face in all types of organizations. We all know that finding innovative solutions to difficult problems is a critical business challenge, and this book will help equip you to bring your most open, optimistic, and creative self to the task.*

*With insightful examples and practical exercises for use with your teams, this is an actionable playbook for making a real difference in the culture of your organization. Yes, and … perhaps even in your personal life as well."*
—**Chris Price, President, Price Leadership Group**

# Previous Works

*Improv To Improve Healthcare: A System for Creative Problem-Solving*

*Channeling Florence Nightingale: Integrity, Insight, Innovation*

*Good Things Come In Small Packages: I Was A Preemie*

*My Mom Is A Nurse*

*My Grandma Is A Nurse*

*Micropremature Babies: How Low Can You Go?* (film)

# Foreword

We face more disruption right now than at any other time in history. It's been happening for decades: globalism; advancing technology; political, social, and cultural upheaval; and more. But the past few years have *really* turned up the heat. The scope, pace, and intensity of change are unprecedented.

The recent pandemic caused major disruptions across most industries. While most organizations have struggled in at least some ways, others have had to almost rebuild from the ground up. They've had to rethink everything about how they operate; who they partner with; and how, where, and when their employees work.

One big consequence, of course, is the Great Resignation. Employees have experienced a mass awakening around what's most important in life. They've gotten very focused on what they want from their jobs. Businesses are scrambling to reinvent their ecosystems in a way that puts employees at the center.

So how do we find our footing in the whirlwind of change? How do we make decisions in the face of so many unknowns? How do we lead in the swirl of chaos? *We improvise.*

When I learned there was a book on using improv skills in leadership, I was delighted. It is such a timely topic. Dr. Candy Campbell builds a strong case for using the principles of improv to help us become more comfortable taking the kinds of creative risks we need to take in business. This makes perfect sense—and it's a skill that's never been more needed than it is right now.

Candy talks about why it's so vital for leaders to be able to move fluidly as circumstances change and adapt to problems as they arise. I agree. In my own businesses and in the organizations I work with, I'm more and more convinced of the great need for just-in-time leadership. Leading in the moment has never been a more essential skill. Sometimes we have to make decisions quickly. We need to know when to own and when to delegate, when to solve and when to facilitate, when to push and when to step back, when to hold a coaching conversation and when to let it go.

In short, leaders need to know what leadership looks like *for that moment*. And it may not be what it looked like a week ago, or a day ago, or even an hour ago. This ability to shift when shifting is called for is the heart and soul of improv.

While I was really impressed with all of the book's improv principles and enjoyed reading about them, several resonated on a personal level.

Number 2 is "Risk being imperfect." I've always found that perfectionism is a major barrier to progress. In life and in business, when we aren't willing to risk mistakes, nothing meaningful can happen. We miss opportunities. Also, when we can't risk showing our humanness and vulnerability, we can't connect with others. As counterintuitive as it may seem, imperfection is the path to growth and change.

Number 4 is "Be helpful." As discussed in my book *The Calling*, people who choose health care as a profession have a great desire to be useful and helpful. This is actually true in many industries. There are many different types of callings. When we can tap into that internal desire to be useful and helpful, we can help people leverage it to serve others and build strong relationships.

I really love number 7, which is "Be thankful; you have what you need." I've written many times on what a powerful force gratitude is, both in building positive workplace cultures and generating personal success and happiness. I appreciate how Candy connects gratitude to the notion of abundance ("you have what you need") and talks about how this mindset shift empowers us to be spontaneous, creative, and proficient at solving problems.

Finally, number 9 is "Look and listen to understand, not to respond." This one gets to the heart of what leaders need to do in order to connect with employees in a meaningful way. Building and nurturing strong relationships is the highest task of a leader, and to do our job of engaging and inspiring employees, we need to know what's going on with them. That means building conversations where we seek to deeply listen into the fabric of our cultures and workdays.

Candy does a wonderful job of framing serious business topics in a fresh and engaging way. Improv tends to be inherently light and funny, which makes it a welcome respite from the stress and anxiety so many of us face daily.

The book is filled with creative exercises and activities your team will love. These are extremely valuable, because people learn by doing. (This would be a great training book as it forces people to get out of their comfort zones and interact with others in unpredictable situations—sort of like work and life itself!)

The power of improv thinking is that it helps companies navigate uncertainty. A pandemic showed us that many organizations struggle with this. Yet we need to prepare ourselves for future disruptions. The virus may be receding but another one, or a different type of crisis, will surely replace it. This is a given. There will always be something. Candy's approach gives us not just the skills but also the mindset to shift quickly and effectively to meet new circumstances as they arise.

It's my hope you'll enjoy *Improv to Improve Your Leadership Team* as much as I did. I am grateful to creative thinkers like Candy who challenge us to learn and grow in ways we may never have considered.

**Quint Studer, Healthcare Solutions Group, Author, *The Calling: Why Healthcare Is So Special***

# The Improv Principles

1. Accept all offers.
2. Risk being imperfect.
3. Avoid Yes/No questions.
4. Be helpful.
5. Silence the Inner Editor.
6. Be adventurous.
7. Be thankful; you have what you need.
8. Actions speak louder than words.
9. Look and listen to understand, not to respond.
10. Focus on your partner.
11. Follow the Story Spine and be changed.
12. Treat others like you want to be treated.

# Preface

## Why I Wrote This Book
(and why you need it)

*"It was a stark and dormy night ... "* that's the beginning line of one of my signature stories.

It was 1995 when I uttered that mis-spoken phrase, while onstage performing with the improv and stand-up comedy troupe I cofounded in the San Francisco Bay area. The audience chortled when they heard it, as it began the scene using their suggestion of "an emotion," which was simply the word, "scary."

That night, that scene, or what happened because of that scene, changed my life. Literally.

Something unusual happened during that scene, which (thankfully) has never occurred to me since. While three of our troupe were onstage, making it up as we went along, our fourth actor was backstage, waiting for a possible *call* to enter the scene. He was thirsty. He grabbed his cup from the tray on a bookshelf, took a drink, and as he put it down, he accidentally missed the tray.

We all heard the loud CRASH.

We three stopped still onstage, frozen. (It was a *scary* scene, after all.)

One of us said a line that had people doubled-up with laughter. (Oh, how often I wished we could remember what he said! Sadly, none of our gigs were filmed, so it lives in my mind as another one of those fun experiences that ALWAYS seems to happen when we perform improv.)

Back to that night.

Afterward, we had the usual group of fans come up and congratulate us on an exhilarating show and a few people (there was always at least one person) asked if we "planned any of it ... especially that CRASH?!"

Our answers were always the same: I said, "Nope, that's the beauty of improv!"

"You never know what you'll get," said my actor friend.

The skeptic cocked his head, "Well, ya coulda had some plants sitting on the audience …"

But we didn't. Ever. Why would we? That would take away half the fun!

After those folks turned to leave, a nice-looking gentleman came forward. He looked pensive.

"Ok," he nodded, "I get that you didn't plan anything tonight. But what I saw up there was … how should I call it … a *transformation.* You spontaneously adapted to a problem … and solved it. You think you could come *transform* my engineers?"

Turns out, Michael (not his real name) was a leader of a start-up software company in Silicon Valley, and they were in trouble. Michael shared that he thought the head-butting was slowing down work and someone had just quit because of "toxic" atmosphere. Could we help? "Teach them how to park their egos and play nice?"

Coincidentally, of the four of us improvers, I was the one who had a BA in Theatre/Acting and minor in education … and some familiarity with curriculum development. So, Michael's question led to the first time I ever taught applied improvisational principles to a business audience.

And guess what?

Michael required his team of eight engineers (plus himself) to show up and take part in that workshop day. As we began, I noticed a LOT of them had their arms folded against their chest. Many of them clearly resented being there.

In my mind, that day was a grand experiment: Would businesspeople find value in this work?

As an actor, I'd taken improv classes for years. The emphasis in those classes was different. Always good, but different, because we actors were studying the craft and working to play to an audience.

Happily, after the first round of exercises, the engineers were all laughing and having so much fun, it *was* a different atmosphere, completely.

That was the first time I chose to incorporate applied improvisational exercises (AIEs) not only from theater, but art, music, writing, and dance.

At the day's end, some of the evaluation comments included:

"I came here thinking I'd have role-play [sic] some situation at work and 'make nice' with people I don't really respect and can't stand. WOW.

Wrong. Funny thing, I'm kind shy guy, had fun, made some new friends at work. (I tend to keep to myself.) [sic]"

Also, among the typical short, left-brained-engineer phrases, like "Excellent," and "Great stuff," I chuckled as one person wrote, "YES, and!"

That day, I realized, just as important as the exercises were, the debriefing process was even more-so. Instead of encouraging student's insights and thoughts every few hours (as we often do in acting classes), I made sure to debrief after each exercise, so that the engineers could share frequently. That decision paid off in cementing the lessons learned and accomplished several objectives:

1. Participants learned to listen and respect the thoughts of some people they previously had not wanted to know or listen to.
2. They learned to adapt to situations quickly.
3. They learned to solve problems creatively and spontaneously.
4. They surprised themselves that they were, individually, able to find the FUN in the work.
5. They united as a group because they had FUN, as a group.
6. They spoke up and shared personal insights that created some interesting discussions.
7. They created trusting relationships with people they had worked with and had not really taken the time to *know*.

You can imagine that at days end, they were all convinced that it was one of the BEST, most fun, most effective team-building experiments ever.

In my follow-up calls to Michael, he mentioned that some of the new freedom the engineers found from the improv exercises that had spilled over into their work. They were beginning to solve the problems that seem to spring up daily ... and innovate new solutions! (That company turned around financially and was eventually subsumed by another, large, well-known, Silicon Valley company.)

Years later, in one of my local improv classes, I met a woman engineer who had worked for the company that bought-out the smaller start-up. When she heard how I got my start teaching improv, she said, "That's why I'm here! So many of the company leaders talk about improv ... I thought I'd better check it out!"

As for me, I learned a great lesson that day also:

No matter how much fun it is to be onstage and get some great audience laughs or even a standing ovation, I love teaching applied improvisational exercises even more.

Why?

It's about the feeling of satisfaction that comes when students of any age or stage (I've taught all sorts) begin to see the freedom of opening their minds to a new way of thinking. It's so fulfilling. It's like a feeling of parental pride, realizing I've passed on a really important skill, enabling behaviors that will change lives with their ability to communicate better, both professionally and personally.

So it is with that backstory, dear Reader, that I welcome you to begin what I hope will be a new way of thinking.

This book contains some principles and exercises to assist you to remold yourself and your teams in what we call, *The Improv Mindset*. I propose that this method of thinking will not only change your workplace, but as heightened creativity also inspires better problem-solving and innovation (if you practice), it will change your life … personally as well as professionally.

I invite you to reach out to me on LinkedIn with your comments!

With care,
Dr. Candy Campbell
Chesapeake Beach, MD

# Acknowledgments

I realize what I'm about to say may date this book, but it is important for historical significance: it's been a tough two years for all of us. During that time, I moved cross-country and began a new life. Like most of us, I've tried to continue some semblance of normality, online.

I am evermore thankful for my friends in the National Speakers Association, especially the Northern California and the DC Chapters, who kept up virtual meetings and shared knowledge of how to become early adaptors of creating an in-home studio and virtually presenting as professional speakers at home. This includes a mastermind group of movers and shakers who are always ready with an idea to solve a problem. Thank you!

Of course, I must not forget those instructors who so graciously imparted their improv knowledge to me in the days when I ventured into the realm of stand-up comedy and improv in the San Francisco Bay area: Sue Walden (ImprovWorks), Bay Area Theatre Sports (BATS), American Conservatory Theatre (ACT), and my three chums who asked me to join them in cofounding the first improv and stand-up troupe in the San Francisco East Bay area, *The Barely Insane Theatre*, Kay DeMartini, Ben Yates, and Jerry Vanderwald. It's because of all of you that I began teaching improv and launched my first solo show.

Kudos and thanks to Quint Studer of the Studer Family of Companies for the Foreword, to my book agent, Nigel Wyatt, for intro to BEP, plus BEP editors Scott Isenberg and Charlene Kronstedt, Mark Jonell for the cover art, VirpiOinonen of *businessillustrator.com* for the cartoons, and Dan Janal, for helping me think through the organization of this, the second book in a series of four on the subject of applied improvisational exercises for various uses.

Of course, I'm always thankful for family and friends who have encouraged me along the way.

You know who you are!

With kindness,
Candy Campbell
March 2022

# PART ONE
# The WHY?

Cartoon by Virpi/BusinessIllustrator.com

# CHAPTER ONE

# What Kind of Leader Are You?

*All the world's a stage and all the men and women merely players.*
*They have their entrances and their exits,*
*And one man in his time plays many parts.*
*—Shakespeare, As You Like It, Act 2, sc. 7*

## All the World's a Stage

Likely, you are familiar with this famous Shakespearean monologue.

In it, Shakespeare reiterates a common theme from this play. In short, he's saying, we're all the same, no matter if high born or low born; we're all just folks. Indeed, we may have a calendar of daily events to check, but none of us wakes up with an actual script of how our day is going to go.

In that regard, Shakespeare might as well have said *"Life is improv."*

Are you aware of the danger of what he said?

At that time, as Shakespeare was not of the aristocracy, but a *commoner*, and to suggest that we are all cut from the same cloth was what the Brits would dub, a cheeky statement. As the monarchy were considered to be chosen by God to rule, to even suggest opposition to their divine right would be considered treason. It is likely (although the records are scarce, so we don't know for sure), Shakespeare presented this play before James I, his patron, who had the ability to imprison him (or worse) immediately, if His Highness felt insulted or, indeed, threatened.

However, Shakespeare was wise in this regard, in that he hedged his bet by placing the ideas in a pastoral-type comedy (farmers were considered ignorant and often the butt of aristocratic humor) and in the mouth of the character of *The Fool*.

Why would he do that?

Recall, in Shakespeare's time, certain comic characters, like The Fool, had prescribed traits. The Fool was a type of the Royal Court Jester, often silly or cynical, sometimes wise, and in theater, took the shape of peasants who spout common knowledge and dispel untruths. The commoners loved these theatrical characters and the aristocrats laughed along, because The Fool was low-born. Everything he said could be taken lightly, so the King would (hopefully) laugh along and not be inclined to shout, "Off with his head!" Shakespeare was subtly using his artistic license to plant seeds in his aristocratic audience. After all, he was a guild-member of the de facto middle class.

What can we learn from Shakespeare?

Shakespeare was a risk-taker. He was an innovator, who used his platform to subtly and not so subtly encourage the renaissance (literally "rebirth" or "reawakening") way of humanist thinking.

As business leaders, gone are the days when authoritarian bosses ruled like kings from the corner office and barked orders to the underlings. No matter what chaos crosses the global stage, in business, it is now perfectly clear that technology requires even the Big Boss to depend upon a team to work together for the benefit of the company.

There are a few constants that plague leaders, no matter what the industry.

In modern times, the world is going through yet another renaissance of thought. Deeper humanist concerns around diversity, equity, and inclusion have created new titles and departments to evaluate and dispel issues such as bullying, sexism, ageism, racism, and so on.

Furthermore, employees are voting with their feet.

A 2021 survey by Psychology Today found that: "Nearly half of employees (48%) say lack of involvement in decisions contributes to stress in the workplace, a significant increase from the last time this question was asked in 2019 (39%)."[1]

The results are clear: Those who lead as a transactional authority are losing in every business outcome measurement. Those leaders who are willing to lead with excellence and show your authentic self and conduct business as a relational leader, win.

But what's a leader to do to turnaround a culture? You are already burdened with so many responsibilities. You're required to be nimble and quick in terms of managing company operations; you form, oversee, and implement organizational policies; you must ensure stockholder and stakeholder goals are met. How can you possibly take-on one more thing?

I'm so glad you asked!

Are you a risk-taker?

The *premise* of this book is that interprofessional miscommunication is the problem. The *promise* is that if you, as the leader, *are willing* to risk *being authentic and vulnerable* (like Shakespeare and the lady in the cartoon), to speak the truth, and encourage interprofessional communication, you can *tear down walls and build bridges* in your organization with the principles of applied improvisational exercises (*improv games* or AIEs) from the arts.

If you will risk trying something new and possibly uncomfortable, AIEs can become your *secret weapon* to assist you to begin to change your organizational culture from *transactional* to *relational*.

For decades, this method has been used to assist leaders to create a culture of safety in their organizations, so that employees feel confident that the risk of speaking up is no longer a threat.

Before we dive in, a caveat: If you want to learn how to bring a culture of safety to an organization, it starts with knowing your purpose. My assertion is that as leaders, we have a kind of *noblesse oblige* to think deeply about how our actions affect others, which includes everyone, not merely the shareholders or those who outrank us. Hence, taking a page from Socrates' philosophy (i.e., the unexamined life is worthless); it all starts with *you*.

Perhaps you thought about your purpose a long time ago, when you were in school or just starting out in business. My belief is that leaders need to revisit their personal leadership purpose often, to keep on track. Here are some assumptions:

- If you want people to work hard and make your company great to reflect on your great leadership, you're off-kilter.
- If you want to help people in your organization to become their best selves, you will succeed in your quest to be a better leader.

- If you seek to do the right thing, for yourself, your family, and your company, because those behaviors make you the kind of leader nobody wants to leave, then your company can become the place where everybody wants to work.

Let's explore that idea.

## Exercise 1a

If you haven't thought about that for a while, I suggest you take a break, go take a walk, or find a quiet place, and ask yourself:

- Why am I doing this work?
- If I died tomorrow, would my leaders and employees be *grieved* or *relieved*?
- Do I have my priorities correct?
- Am I willing to learn to be a better version of myself?

Perhaps you didn't expect this book to be so personal? That begs this next question ...

## Who Are You?

(And How Much is MIS-Communication Costing Your Business?)

## Your Leadership Role

The British Monarch, the U.S. President, Elon Musk ... and the kid next door who mows your lawn.
   All are leaders.

Have you had leadership thrust upon you?
Do you find yourself overworked and seemingly ineffective?
Are you an enthusiastic leader who seeks to learn how to become better?
Have you wondered how you could "up your game" and *develop* into
   a leader?
This book is for you.

Let's talk fundamental truths and sort it out from there.

Looking back a few thousand years, consider the Greek tradition that tells us, being human equates to being an *individual*. The Roman tradition flips the idea a bit, in that the word for *person* (persona) equates to *the role that we play in life*. (Since Aristotle, theater has been utilized to put forth ideas about how we live.) As Shakespeare noted, everyone has a role to play in life. Your successful role, as a leader, hinges less on the title and more with how your leadership affects the body politick of your organization.

## WIIFM ... AMC?

You likely picked up this book because you need help. You need solutions. You either have problems with employee disengagement, poor retention rates, or both, and you want to know how to avoid them, as the buck stops with you. You're wary of some crazy method that sounds too obtuse. You want results.

I get that. You're thinking, "What's in it for me ... and my company?"

Before you put away the idea of improv for business as just a kooky attempt at teaching comedy, let me explain that applied improv is NOT comedy, per se.

True, the workshops create a lot of laughter, but it's not based on jokes. The delight you'll experience emanates from the honest reactions of participants who are surprised by the joy of *being in the moment*, getting in touch with their *inner artist*,[2] as author Julia Cameron would say, building trust in relationships, and spontaneously solving the organic problems that occur in partners, groups, or onstage.

But before we delve into the applied improvisational exercises, and to make this learning personal, let's ponder your recollections about your relationship with past leaders.

## Culture Trumps Everything

### Exercise 1b

Take a moment to reflect. (You might want to journal your results.)

- Please recall your worst-ever boss. You know, the one whose face popped into your mind when you read that.
- Now, think of an employment situation that did not have the outcome you desired … and you left, willfully or not. Were the two memories connected?

Perhaps, the situation was due to your own shortcomings, negligence, or failure to act? We hope not, but that's always a possibility. (If so, good news; you're here now, reading this book to learn how to be the leader you want to be!)

Perhaps, it was a simple downsizing or a relocation that predicated the change? (Life happens!)

Perhaps, unforeseen physical or other challenges caused you to be unable to continue in that position? (Ditto above!)

Whatever the reason, think back to the time of separation from that entity.

- How were you treated?

Recall the kind of leadership that created any negative image you carry.

- How did that make you feel?
- How does it make you feel now, as you recall it?

(Note: If the leader who counseled or showed you the door was a person of integrity, who understood relationships, they should have given you grace to leave with respect.)

Now, think of the opposite, about the *best* boss you ever had.

- This person showed an ability to relate to people who far exceeded your expectations.
- This was no transactional leader who expected you to put in eight hours and earn your paycheck, doing mindless work, no.
- This leader appreciated the personal touch you brought to the business, no matter what your position.

Correct?

Now think of that boss and that situation:

- Where were you?
- How old were you?
- Was that person older or younger than you?
- What story do you have that exemplifies the kind of leadership you experienced that you want to emanate?

I hope that you have many more positive leader-memories than negative ones. Likely, not.

Sadly, most employees who exit a company give their bosses low scores and equate poor leadership as one of the main reasons they choose to leave.[3]

## The REAL Cost of Employee Turnover

### The Trickle-Down Effect

Aside from disgruntled employees who get saddled with more work when their colleague leaves (and that can foment more problems down the line), what is the real COST of employee separation and turnover?

First, there's the up-front financial cost of orienting/training a new employee. You know that those costs are worrisome on the grand scale. According to the November 2021 Industry Training report,[4] large businesses spent an average of $17.7 million, mid-sized companies spent $1.3 million, and small companies spent $341,505, a year, on training.

Couple that with the cost of replacing an employee, according to Forbes (2021),[5] costs range from one-half to two times an employee's annual salary.

In other words, if you have 100 employees with an average salary of $60,000, your replacement cost could be anywhere from $30,000 to $120,000, *per resignation!*

Taking it a step further, if your company suffered the employee resignations of the 2021 average of 30 percent, your company would incur a range of expense from $999,000 to $3.9 million to replace them. Yikes!

But wait!

If you decide NOT to address the issue of employee DIS-engagement in the workplace (insert reams of boring statistics that pepper the news every quarter), you KNOW what will happen. Yes, you will continually go through that hire-train-rehire cycle, like Sisyphus pushing the rock uphill.

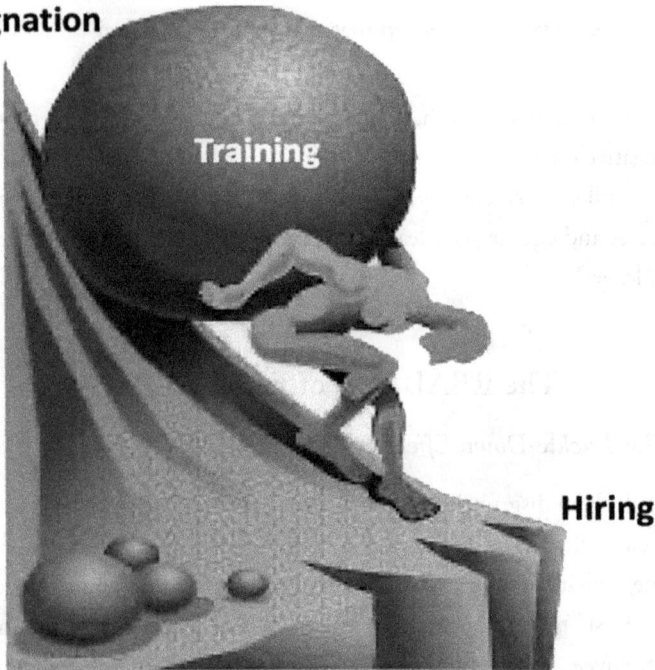

## The Causes of Problems in the Workplace

What does the latest research tell us? Diversity, Equity, and Inclusion (DEI) have come to light, finally, as very important to strategically accost, and yet, the research shows that issue is not the only variable that needs to be addressed.

Employees who leave, do so for two main reasons (I've selected three references, but there are many):

1. The culture of the workplace is not fulfilling (or just downright toxic)[6]
2. Employees don't feel a sense of belonging[7,8]

In fact, as this goes out to the publisher, more than 4 million employees between the years 2020 and 2022 have QUIT! (The numbers don't include employees who are thinking about leaving.)

What makes people stay?

Surveys show employees stay because of several concerns, including:

- opportunity for professional development,
- versatile hours,
- hybrid workspaces,
- but moreover, the overarching theme of *culture*.

How do employees define a positive culture today? The DEI aspects include specifics about managers who are approachable and, most of all, a culture where employees are known, respected, and heard.[9,10]

It sounds so simple.

If you're a leader of any title, you already know that the onus for employee engagement rests mainly on managers, since they are the people who speak most often to employees.

(Obviously, in customer service industries, your front-line employees effectively *manage* clients, but their managers are the people who *manage* them; it's their job to create the sense of belonging.)

This book is meant to be a tool for you, dear Reader-Leader, to use as a first step in the direction of designing a *culture of safety* in the workplace, both in-person or in-hybrid places.

### Culture of Safety

How can you recognize a safe company culture? Does it include the *Joy at Work* program or *Work–Life Balance* movements?

The short answer is that exorcising a toxic culture and providing and nurturing a culture of safety for any industry has less to do with surprise clown-nose gags, a joke-a-day, or yoga, bubble baths, and so-called self-care.

Moreover, in some prescribed, happiness-seeking environments, managers are expected to be aware of risk factors and monitor for signs of disengagement and distress. Unfortunately, that sort of *lurking* behavior appears often like *invasion of privacy* and creates other headaches for HR and Risk Management departments.

People either feel safe to speak their minds (respectfully, of course), offer suggestions, and know they are respected in return ... and heard ... or not.

You won't have to look very far to see this practice gone wrong, horribly wrong.

### Beware Checking the Box to Provide Positive Culture

Newton's third law of motion explains that to every action there will be an equal and opposite reaction. That statement is true for human behavior as well as for physical objects.

Sometimes organizations are clueless as to what to do with the new directives about the need to retain employees and improve customer experience. They know they need to check the box that they have complied with some attempt to quell the problem, but don't know what to do with the issue, and are often strapped with cash concerns about creating a new line item in the budget to pay for any new program. In addition, leadership sometimes fails to comprehend the effects of a new policy.

Examples abound.

Recently, I visited a retail store where the overhead music piped in the song, "Happy," on a continuous loop. I like that song, but after twice through, when I noticed it repeated, I looked at the salesperson and asked, "Do they play that a lot?"

"All day," she returned, rolling her eyes and shaking her head. "I wanna rip the speakers off the wall!"

Clearly, you cannot legislate emotions.

Another personal example is when I worked as an administrator for a large government agency. I had a large case load of client representatives to manage. I made it my business to get to know as many of them as possible.

When I called on them (with permission), I took a photo, printed it out in my office, made an info card for each one in my desk organizer, and included some interesting facts (number of kids, things in common, birthday, etc.). This proved to be a great icebreaker and relationship-builder.

Others in the office thought that activity was a colossal waste of time and joked about it.

Since it was my job to keep the reps compliant with the laws pertaining to their work, it seemed only natural to have a friendly relationship with each. (Besides, I like people and I missed the clinical aspect of work in the Neonatal Intensive Care Unit [NICU].)

The advantage was that I was able to help solve problems of sorting through pages of legal requirements before they became headaches for the client organizations, by answering questions and providing compliance education for the reps in ways they could understand. (Ah, the benefits of having taught school!) Again, others in the office chided me for "hand-holding" the reps.

Result? My monthly reports showed the best compliance rates the agency had ever seen. (When I moved on from that job, I received flowers, candy, cards, and gifts from reps who said they would miss me!)

Interesting that in our actual agency office, employee turnover rate was between 18 and 20 percent. (This was way before COVID-19!)

In response to these alarming numbers (and to quell the retreat), the state overseers sent the Director a "Suggestion Box." She was instructed to mount it in a prominent place.

The Director decided to put it right by the water fountain, between the lavatories.

The attached sign read, "JOY AT WORK. Suggestions."

Let's just say the suggestion box did not create a joyous atmosphere there, nor quell the retreat, to put it mildly.

One Friday, at end of day, the Director asked me to come into her office. She had the Suggestion Box and its contents strewn across her desk.

"Good thing I put down some paper towels over the top of my desk before I opened this," she mused.

I looked down and saw an assortment of items, including some scraps of paper, a used tissue, a dust bunny, and a paper clip.

"Could be worse," she clipped. "Read this."

She handed me a couple scraps of paper with some profanity scribbled on them.

One slip of paper said, "What we need is more help and more money. That would bring me enough joy not to blow this place."

"What are you supposed to do with this?" I queried.

"Hellifino, rhino," she laughed.

The hierarchy had not included instructions on how to address the comments, only that the box would be hung in a prominent spot where all could access it. (Check box.)

We mused over the contents occasionally, when she cleaned it out, since mostly the box was empty (except for a steady stream of used tissues and paper clips). She never received an actionable comment, although she mentioned that the administration encouraged anyone to speak up using the Suggestion Box (to keep their identity private), or they could make an appointment with her.

(Note: The Director kept her office door closed most of the time, "to avoid my time being hijacked by brown-nosers and whiners," and required her secretary to make appointments; NO drop-in discussions.)

Ironically, soon after, it was revealed by the Director of the State Accounting Department that the semiannual inventory of supplies was "out of balance" (indicating office supplies were missing without proper assignment). Our Director called for another staff meeting, and everyone was warned that *pilfering* was grounds for dismissal.

The next week, the Director stopped me in the hall and said, "Did you move the Suggestion Box?"

I didn't even notice it was gone, but someone had removed it. We found it in the dumpster, outside.

This story shows another inept attempt to improve employee engagement and retention rates.

I bothered to relate these examples, to show that this problem is SO common, you probably have some awful stories, too!

### The Risks of Creating a Culture of Safety

Helping usher in a culture of safety so managers understand how to create and maintain it requires that personal *risk* of being authentic and vulnerable. Perhaps, you'll need a willingness to look a little silly at times, in order to become a leader who is interested in more than your status symbols and profit and loss. It's about recommitting yourself as a *leader* in the larger sense.

Yes, that may sound a little woo-woo, but hear me out as we dissect the idea.

One thing for sure: a *culture of safety* for the workplace cannot solely be accomplished by sitting behind your desk with the door shut, and it's more complicated than leaving your door open to occasional impromptu conversation.

This philosophy of how leaders and their managers should behave in the workplace differs hugely from the dinosaur days, when leaders were told to close their office doors, make employees come to you with questions/concerns, never fraternize with employees, and appear a certain way (i.e., neutral-colored, expensive suits; drive the latest car; conservative hairstyle, don't walk around lest someone engage you in needless conversation, ask a difficult question, or confront you, etc.).

The list of top-rated places to work changes yearly, but those who manage to knock down silos embrace a culture of safety and concentrate on what leaders need to deliver the best *employee experience* so that, by extension, the customer will have the best *client experience.* Just look at companies that have weathered any crisis for examples that creating a culture of safety is smart business, whether you measure it in employee retention, happy customers, or escalating profits, even during a global crisis.

As a leader, you can't legalize joy in the workplace with a policy, but you can crack a joke at your own expense occasionally, to create the mood of fun, from the top down. Think of it as romancing the workplace. What makes you look forward to going to the office or doing whatever work needs to be done? Likely, part of the anticipation (and the fun) comes from the connections you have with others.

Nevertheless, at the sharp end of the stick, where the actual product or service is completed, when one person leaves, someone must pick up the slack and that is stressful. Usually, the highest producing/functioning employee will be saddled with extra work, until the position is filled. Then, how does that high-functioning employee feel? Overworked? Disgruntled? Unappreciated? And how do those negative employee feelings lead to other behaviors?

Much research has been conducted about the results of employee feelings of negativity in the workplace and how that affects other employees, the greater culture, and the workflow.[11]

As a leader, you set the tone for the culture. The responsibility rests on your shoulders and it begins with your *personal purpose.*

# What Kind of Business Are You In?

### Complex Adaptive Systems (CAS) and Your Personal Purpose

You may have heard, "Business is just business. It's not personal."

I beg to differ.

Organizations that embrace such a philosophy forget one key fact: Leaders are in the *people* business, no matter what service or product they provide.

Even if you are in a product-producing industry, your products depend upon people to handle the machines. Machines are complex systems (CS), but people are complex adaptive systems (CAS). If a machine part malfunctions, the assembly line stops. If one body part is damaged or broken, the CAS will automatically compensate as much as possible, until it can flex no more: on the inside and outside, we're in a continual state of flux.

Hence, people are complicated, and your business is definitely a CAS.

So, if you want to create a workplace that retains employees and creates raving fans out of your clients, people need you, the leader, to be more of a mentor-coach than an authoritarian figure, who only dispenses orders and discipline.

Such a modern leadership practice goes by various names, for example, Transformational Leadership, Servant Leadership, and the list goes on. Whatever the moniker, the point is the same: *People need leaders who are effective and who show they care.*

Tall order, to be sure, and it hinges upon your *personal purpose.*

Certainly, you leaders of large organizations will be unable to act as mentor-coach to all your employees, so that is not the assumption of this book.

However, it is the intention of this tome that you will be able to enact positive organizational cultural changes, if you are clear about your personal *raison d'etre* and adopt the improv principles into your work. (If you haven't completed Exercises 1a and 1b, please do so now.)

## Organizational Philosophy and the Bottom Line

### Soft Skills and EI

Typically, business runs on cold-hard facts and the bottom-line numbers, profit and loss, right?

Why all the fuss about so-called, soft skills?

Enter psychologist and author Daniel Goleman, whose first book in 1995 reflected seminal research on *emotional intelligence* (EI) and *social intelligence* (SI),[12] reflects that these often overlooked soft skills are linked to a culture of safety, self-confidence, better teamwork, creativity, spontaneity, adaptability, and increased ability to problem-solve, it encourages innovation, joy at work, and the gold-standard of organizational monitoring, *employee retention* ... and THAT creates good communication.

But how do you, a leader, help create a culture of safety so that curiosity is encouraged, ideas freely exchanged, and office politics, gossip, and backbiting is reduced or eradicated?

### The Neuroscience

In the first book in this series about improvisation from the arts, *Improv to Improve Healthcare,* I went deep into the research on this topic, since change in health care is based on evidence-based research.

I'm not saying that you, business leader, aren't interested in the science. I also know you don't like to waste time going down rabbit trails. You want the basics. So, I'll give a brief overview here and refer you to that book, should you desire more information.

In a nutshell, here's the gist: Humans react powerfully to both a smile or a frown, seen even 10 feet away.[13,14] If you perceive that either expression was aimed at you, your brain will percolate with one of two very specific reactions. Either you'll feel happy, energized, and/or more creative (when the happy hormones kick-in) or you'll feel the opposite (possibly frustrated, depressed, forgetful, even angry) when the corticosteroids or unhappy hormones are triggered.

Furthermore, cognitive behavioral studies tell us that *humans learn best when they are having fun.*[15]

We can observe that in any CAS, as problems increase, frustrations increase, then teamwork decreases, which slows workflow. How long before one employee quits and the cycle repeats?

Makes sense, right?

On the contrary, if the overall culture of safety prevails, everyone is on the watch for problems, since (nonlethal) problems are viewed as opportunities to flex and innovate.

With the study of neuroscience, one thing is for sure: creativity is like a muscle that needs to be exercised.

### Quelling the Left Brain

Before we begin the process of the group improv exercises, I want to introduce you to a helpful method to inspire creativity.

Quite a lot has been written on creativity and the difference between left and right brain, most famously by M. Csikszentmihalyi,[16] in his work on *finding creative flow*, and Betty Edwards, in her ground-breaking book for artists, *Drawing on the Right Side of the Brain*.[17]

Edwards outlines a practice to engage the area of the right brain, to sort of get the creative juices flowing. It's insightful and I use these types of examples in my workshops.

Please try these three exercises at home before you introduce the exercises to your team. They are fun and you might amaze yourself!

The following exercises are examples and demonstrate how we can quickly move from left-to-right brain, to access more creative thinking.

### Exercise 1c—Optical illusion 1

### Directions

Stare at the object for a few seconds. Do you see both the vase and the two faces?

If you cannot switch from one to another, try closing one eye, then the other.

If that doesn't work, try looking away for a few seconds, then look back at the image.

If you can "flip" from one view to another, congratulations; your right and left brain are working together in harmony!

Practice again with another one:

*Exercise 1d—Optical Illusion 2*

**Directions: (Same as Above)**

*Debrief*

1. Were you able to see both the faces/vase and rabbit/duck figures relatively soon?
2. If not, did you feel frustrated because you were having trouble?
3. Were you intrigued by this experiment?
4. After you were able to switch back and forth from one image to the other, how did that make you feel?

5. What are your takeaways from this exercise?

6. Journal (or share) your responses.

Here's another right-brain exercise to get you really out of your comfort zone! By the time you're finished with these sorts of right-brain stimulating exercises, you should be able to feel the subtle changes.

The image you see here is upside down. That's not a mistake, it's part of the fun.

If the dominant left brain observes a thing right-side up, it goes quickly to work, categorizing and matching the images, naming them, and storing information about them.

When we turn an image upside down, our left brain becomes confused. We may see shadows and shapes, but our left brain will be stymied into a *cognitive shift*. This gives our right brain a chance to take over and look at even a familiar image in a new way. Dare I say, invent a new way of seeing the image?

## Exercise 1e—Drawing Upside Down

### Directions: (Take ~ 10 minutes)

1. Look at the image upside down ONLY.

2. Take a blank sheet of paper and a pen or pencil.

3. Find a quiet place. (Play soft music, if it won't distract you.)

4. *Focus on the center spot of the image only,* taking in the lines, angles, and random shapes.

5. Note where the lines start and end in relation to each other and the edges of the paper. Think to yourself, "Here's a curvy line that goes that way, crosses over there ...." And so on.

6. START to draw at the TOP of your paper.

7. Don't name the parts of the body to yourself as you recognize them; just concentrate on the lines and spaces as you draw.

8. Keep working down the page until you get to the end.

9. Don't worry about being perfect, it's not about fine art. It's about concentrating on the lines; just go with the flow of a new experience.

Painting of old woman in chair:    Inverted drawing based on painting

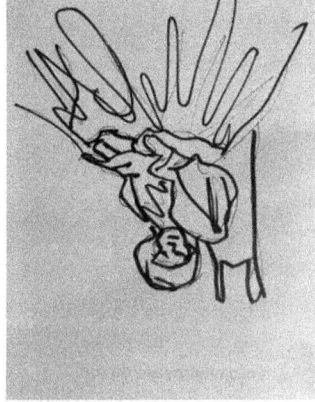

## *Debrief*

- Now, turn the drawing right side up. Your thoughts?
- If you're doing this with your group, allow everyone to hold up their drawings.
- Discuss thoughts about this process.
- What are your takeaways? Your aha-moments?

## How to Get the Most Out of This Book

You've made it through the preparation. Good work!

Now that you've completed the first exercises, you are ready for Stage 2 learning.

The first key to using this method of applied improvisational exercises is to take a deep breath, set your mind at ease, and settle into this very moment, wherever you are.

- Be still and listen.
- Reread the 12 improv principles I've listed in the front matter of this book.
- Chapters Three to Ten cover one or more of those principles, which are key concepts for personal life as improv.
- Then, look at the exercises within each chapter.

- Imagine how they will help to get conversations and discussions flowing in your group. If you're doing virtual meetings, you might even do some of the ice-breaker partner exercises in break-out rooms.
- Have fun with it!

This book presents you with a program to counter that negativity and create a new culture in your workplace. A helpful solution is to inculcate a culture of ideas-exchange that begins with these principles that create what we devotees like to call, *the Improv Mindset*. The active ingredient, the yeast in the dough, if you please, is the practice of AIEs from the arts.

Based on my decades teaching this modality, my experience is, if you make the decision to work with a skilled improv facilitator, your results will be far *beyond* your expectations.

Now go forth and *be ready to be changed!*

# Notes

PART TWO

# Applying the Improv Principles

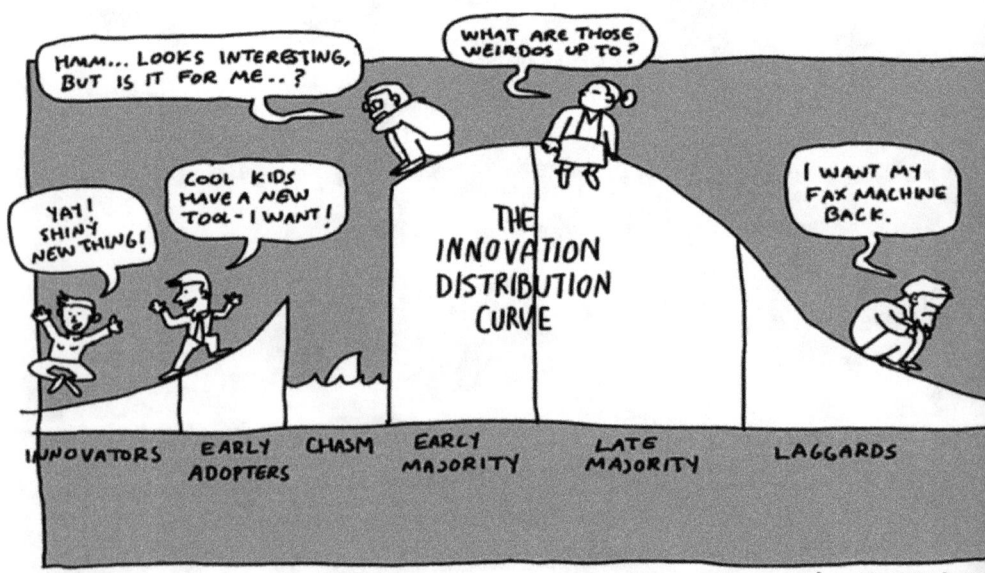

Cartoon by Virpi/BusinessIllustrator.com

# CHAPTER TWO

# Adaptability

*The same sort of thinking that caused the problem will not solve it.*
—Albert Einstein

*Principle 1: Accept all offers*
*Principle 2: Risk being imperfect*

## Barn-Raising

During COVID-19, I moved to the rural south of Maryland. The area has four seasons, which is surprisingly enjoyable alternative to the California drought-ridden landscape, where I lived for many years. It is also lush and green and full of historical remnants, for example, "George Washington slept here," and so on.

Notwithstanding the area's rich agrarian history, the number of old barns dotting the landscape surprised me, as many are still standing after hundreds of years. They stand like ghostly memories.

These days, most barns are built with a crane and a small crew. But not so long ago (and in some communities in the United States today), barn raising was a community event. Farming families needed at least one barn and/or may need to enlarge it, or to restore one that had been damaged.

Recently, on an outing to the Lancaster, PA, area, we stopped at an Amish village and saw, among so many quaint practices, a video showing an actual modern-day barn raising. It was a testament to the necessary planning and skill required to create such a bastion of the farming community.

Barns are large, expensive, and require a lot of material. By necessity, neighbors and friends chipped in their time and talent to literally raise the barn walls. In the spirit of comradery, reciprocity was assumed whenever possible. Whole families came together for a few days to prepare and make sure the event was a success, including the feast at the end to celebrate. It takes a village, after all!

Similarly, accepting the challenge of starting a new business or remodeling the infrastructure of an existing one is a little like the concept of barn raising: Once you accept that the project is important, before you can begin, it requires planning. Since learning anything new in a group requires effort, as in barn raising, we don't just launch into the actual improv exercises without preparing ourselves for the work.

So, leader-friend, you're not expected to be able to raise this new project, to nurture a new culture of safety, alone. You will need excellent and appropriate tools, and that's what this book is all about.

Although I had many years of experience facilitating applied improvisational learning workshops in various businesses, my doctoral proof of concept research was completed with interprofessional groups at Stanford's Lucille Packard Children's Hospital (LPCH).

Since that time, much more has been written about the efficacy of this method, thanks to celebrities like Alan Alda.[1] (After he became a patient, he realized how badly healthcare needs better communication and quite literally, a culture of safety to improve patient safety.)

Meanwhile, in terms of Roger's diffusion of innovation theory,[2] the small business community, in the United States, has been innovators and early adopters, since the 1990s, in many areas, especially Silicon Valley.

Congratulate yourself for being an innovator in your business community, or at least, an early adopter!

### Acceptance: Offers and Imperfection

I trust you are the type of person who adopts a positive mindset before you begin anything new?

Good.

Just like in any new endeavor, you'll need positive buy-in from your leadership teams in order to be successful at this work. I promise, it won't be difficult once you understand the process.

When you utilize these improvisational principles from the arts, your overall success relies heavily on your ability to keep positivity focused.

Of course, sometimes you may say "No …" or argue in improv, but over-all, you will move the conversation, the scene, and/or the relationship forward, if you accept all offers.

Remember: To create a safe space for these workshops, you should avoid creating exercises or scenes that encompass your actual workplace.

Why?

It helps participants practice the principles without the risk of … (fill in the blank with many reasons people hide their real feelings). It also diffuses any resistance they might have if mandated to attend. Role-playing office or workplace scenarios can be very uncomfortable, very fast.

Again, the goal is to *create a safe space to learn and grow,* so we will **not** be doing work-related role-play.

This may seem counterintuitive, as the goal is to advance communication in your workplace.

Fear not.

Just trust the process; improv is an exercise in being good-natured.[3]

On the improv stage, as in life, you have no predetermined script. You only have an idea of why you might be having a conversation with whomever is there with you.

In most cases, you will be given at least one *suggestion* of a specific time, place, relationship, or emotion attached to the person with whom you share the stage.

You will try to be good-natured and make the best of it. We use the principles as a lynchpin to keep us on track.

Let's start with the fundamental improv concept of *accepting an offer.*

This first principle can be explained by looking at ancient stories, where we often read of gifts presented to kings or *offerings* made to gods.

In improv circles, we say *words are golden.*

Therefore, an *offer* is a *gift*; it is anything another person says to you onstage that endows you with a name, location, an emotion, and so on.

## ACE It!

To remember this, I use the acronym **A-C-E.** (See Glossary for more terminology.)

So, your first job is to:

- *A—accept the offer,* by saying "Yes" to whatever is *offered* to you.

Next, find a way to:

- *C—continue the offer* by saying "Yes, and ..." (or the equivalent) add something that will move the scene forward.

Lastly,

- E—embellish the offer with a statement that gives the scene some detail.

Here's an example of when participants do NOT adhere to Principle 1. The scene: Mac and Jack are planning a fishing trip:

**Mac:** Whew! The sun is up and it's gonna be a lovely day for fishin'!

**Jack:** Yah, but the mosquitos are up, too. I can hear 'em! (Swats his arm) Dang!

**Mac:** Oh, those little blood-suckers! Here, I brought some bug spray.

**Jack:** Yah, thanks, but I'm allergic to that stuff.

**Mac:** OK, we got plenty of time. Let's go back inside and you can grab whatever you usually use?

**Jack:** Yah, but, I dunno. It doesn't do any good. Besides, the sun is so hot already, we'll probably get heatstroke.

**Mac:** I got an extra big straw hat you can use.

**Jack:** How 'bout we stay here and pop a few cold ones, instead?

Hmmm. What's your reaction to that scene? Does it make you sorry for Jack? or Mac?

What a sad friendship. Most of us know a "Yah, but ..." person like Jack, who negates every idea. It sounds like he's agreeing, but he's really not.

Let's try again and have the characters work with the A-C-E principle of saying "Yes, and …" accepting offers, and building on the action.

> **Mac:** Whew! The sun is up and it's gonna be a lovely day for fishin'!
> **Jack:** Yah, and the mosquitos are up, too. I can hear 'em! (Swats his arm) Dang!
> **Mac:** Oh, those little blood-suckers! Here, I brought some bug spray.
> **Jack:** Yah? Oh, thanks, I'm gonna spray it all over, on my fishin' rod, too!
> **Mac:** Really? What do you expect will happen?
> **Jack:** More fish! Last week I sprayed all my equipment—hook, line, and sinker—and I caught 14 trout!
> **Mac:** Whoo-hee! I'm gonna spray all my equipment *and* this big straw hat. We'll have fish jumpin' onto the dock!

Notice when you sense the conversations stall and when they flow. See the difference?

When Jack accepts Mac's offers, the whole scene changes. Jack is still bothered by mosquitoes, but he's found a trade-off that moves the scene forward.

Jack has just demonstrated how positive attitude and Principle 1, "Yes, and …" works to move a conversation forward.

## Necessary Cautions—Let It Go!

There's a saying in business, if you're not frequently failing, you're playing it safe, you're not trying anything new.

Principle 2 is to try something new, and *risk making mistakes*.

We practice, *imperfectly*, with improv exercises so we can improve connection, creativity, and communication. It's in the same way that football players workout by lifting weights and doing agility runs, dancers workout by stretching, leaping, and trying new moves, and musicians workout by playing scales and trying new harmonies.

Since we established that neuroscience teaches, as humans, we learn best when we are having fun, the object is to *play*, by observing, listening, and relating to others.

In this way, we build emotional and social intelligence. The side-product is self-assurance and feeling authentic, in any situation.

(Note: We will separate discrete skills, like learning new software or recalibrating a machine, from other kinds of training. Although, those types of activities might make it into our improv games!)

This is especially important to remember if you work in any *risk-averse* industry, because there, people work very hard to AVOID making mistakes, lest someone gets hurt or dies.

In improv, no one gets hurt. No blood is shed, and no one really dies (although that might appear to happen onstage).

There is another reason we make a big deal out of accepting our mistakes as *gifts* in improv. Our acceptance of imperfection spills over to the subconscious.

According to years of research by The Gallup organization's Clifton Strengthsfinder,[4] there are numerous psychological benefits to focusing on our strengths as opposed to focusing on our weaknesses. The encouragement versus shame philosophy wins every time. (Ask any kindergarten teacher!)

Another caveat: Applied improv exercises do NOT morph into psychodrama or psychotherapy. (Those sorts of therapeutic sessions are conducted with psychotherapists or clinical behavioral psychologists, where childhood experiences are teased from attendees, dramatized, then analyzed to shed light on present behaviors and assist in emotional *break-throughs.* Those sorts of sessions are mainly used as an entry point for care in usually very small groups. They are very private.) This is NOT that. We are not working to trigger anyone to face a particular demon in their past.


### Consider, Connect, and Create

Instead, our goal is to learn to consider all input, connect with others, and create solutions that can transform our relationships. We admit, as equal participants, that *we are imperfect, and that's okay.*

When we acknowledge our inherent fallibility as truth and support each other, we are able to enjoy the freedom to learn together and spon-taneously adapt to situations, which is also the key to great teamwork!

Note: Any participant who balks at admitting this truth (or tries to save face, as it were) will find the loss of control troubling and upsetting.

Those students, especially those with a leadership title, may feel it's their duty to try to *lead* improv conversations (we call that *driving* in improv—see Chapter Five) to a preconceived end. Since the exercises are crafted so everyone is seen and heard, drivers play against the rules.

Other participants err in the opposite direction. Perhaps, because they usually choose to *go along to get along*, they feel stuck and don't know what to say or how to move a relationship forward with anyone they don't know. Never fear, your facilitator will gently ease them into the game.

Some participants may want to give way to preconceived *triggers* to their self-esteem and forfeit the ability to play and grow by shutting down, emotionally. These participants take offense at the rules of any given exercise or whine:

*"I don't want to play this game."*
*"I can't. I didn't get my mocha-latte yet!"*

This is another reason why class preparation of expectations and agreements (SEE AGREEMENTS) is so important!

(Again, your facilitator will work to make everyone feel at ease and nothing will be asked that would purposely embarrass anyone.)

## Won't You Be My Neighbor?

Perhaps it's Pollyannaish to say that strangers are only friends you haven't met yet? I agree with Mr. Rogers on that one, simplistic as it may sound. Indeed, that philosophy is the nexus of what this work is about, and it summarizes the first two principles. Practicing applied improv is a way to learn to play together and feel free enough to *risk looking silly* in front of your peers.

As a leader, you might bristle at the thought of letting down your guard, even for a few minutes. What will they think if they see their leader not taking their work seriously?

My suggestion is for you to engage in the improv training with your leadership team. Don't just mandate a new training and sit back and watch. This one is different!

Together, allow yourselves to experience the nuanced benefits of creating *something out of nothing*, and see how that translates into more creative solutions in the workplace.

Suggestion: After you and your team have experienced the improv training, start with an improv-based brainstorming session. Remember to allow ALL thoughts to be considered, no matter how silly or outrageous, and lead with the question, "What if ...?"

I guarantee that if it is facilitated well, your leadership team will surprise you. (But let's not get ahead of ourselves. Read more about application in Chapter Ten.)

As you introduce the idea of the training to your leadership team, it's likely, many of them are already interested in the improvisational art form. Most will have seen a television show that popularized the comedy aspect. (Explain to them, it's not the same!) Some may have seen an improv theatrical show or some may have been exposed to improv training in their early years.

I'm betting that, with proper facilitation, your leadership team will be able to enthusiastically embrace the beauties of experiential learning. (Harness that enthusiasm so they can be involved in the *train-the-trainer* workshops and certifications for the entire organization, and I promise you won't regret it.)

Now we're ready to begin!

## Improv Workshops—A Taste

### Prepare a Safe Space for Learning

Recall that during the global pandemic, people worked together to keep safe by washing hands, and wearing masks. It was uncomfortable to make these changes, but we were duty bound to become super-vigilant about spreading the virus and/or reducing the risk of being exposed to it. (No wonder when the 1918–1920 pandemic passed, it was followed by the Roaring 20s!)

Although improv classes are not dangerous, some people may feel anxious about attending an improv workshop. Some of the reasons people fear change is because of their fear of embarrassment and risk of recrimination when speaking up in the presence of perceived leaders.[5] Even the idea of improv training is bound to throw some people into an emotionally labile state.

I understand.

Having completed the classical actors' curriculum, before the time when improvisation was a staple of theater training, the mere idea of going onstage with no script seemed terrifying, like tightrope walking without a net! I enjoyed improvisational music and dance and reasoned the transition for those professionals was more natural; they were adept enough to play freely in a new way .... But theater?

Likely, you've felt the same way?

It seemed so impossible; I had no idea what to expect. I tell you, before my first improv class (for actors), I was *nervous*. My stand-up buddy cajoled me, saying "Try one class, just ONE class. You'll be hooked, I know it!" He was right; I did love it, once I put the proverbial toe in the water.

Much of what I do now is modeled on the wonderful acting instructors at some of San Francisco's most famous improv comedy theaters. They were all so patient and explained everything so well, I felt right at ease.

Moreover, the freedom I enjoyed playing improv games spilled over to stand-up, where I continued to perform feeling much more relaxed and authentic onstage. As a matter of fact, my three solo shows were all created using improv principles.

As a side note, I also felt a new self-confidence in my personal life that I hadn't felt for a long time. I hear this often from my students.

Why?

We can accomplish this because employees feel safe enough to take off their *work face* and risk feeling vulnerable enough to be authentic.

How do we help people begin to build authentic relationships with others they may not know or who they have already decided they don't want to know?

### Crucial Beginnings

Here is my blueprint for the preparation part and steps for how we'll use applied improvisational exercises to begin the process of increasing emotional and social intelligence (EI and SI) to practice better communication.

- Open the room 30 minutes prior to the start of the workshop.
- Play some lighthearted, peppy music in the background during the initial gathering and sign-in periods. Music helps set the mood.
- Place a table at the door with printed materials (including Appendix A, Participant/Organizational Release/Liability Forms, etc.) and/or Appendix B, Group Agreement, plus notebooks/pens for journaling exercises.
- Greet each participant and insure they take materials.
- Have water/coffee/tea and or snacks (budget-depending), especially if this is an a.m. start time, to encourage conversation before you begin.
- Do NOT use nametags. (Even if your attendees don't know each other, you will learn everyone's name soon.) The work is best when there are no preconceived names, titles, or positions. Keep the group to 20 or less for best results.

### Ten Minutes Before Workshop Begins

- You (or Assistant) announce that the workshop begins promptly in 10 minutes.
- You are eager to welcome everyone, but first, talk about emergency exits, restrooms, drinking fountains, scheduled breaks, and the importance of being on time.
- Invite participants to use the restroom and get hydrated now in preparation.
- Request participants to complete the release forms, and so on, before the class begins.
- Explain about continuing education credits, IF appropriate.
- Collect all forms before the start.
- Announce that when the music stops, the doors will close, and the class begins.

## Go Time!

Ideally, your assistant can read your short introduction, which states your credentials, and is lighthearted. An example of my introduction might be:

> Friends, our workshop facilitator today is an award-winning actor, author, and filmmaker, who co-founded her own improv company in the San Francisco area in the 1990s, and she's been teaching improv in several countries, to all ages and stages, since 1995. Well, she's an improv actor, so I have no idea what she's going to say. Please welcome, Dr. Candy Campbell.

- Provide a copy of your intro a day in advance and bring a copy printed double-spaced in large font, just in case.
- Ask your introducer to be familiar with it, not embellish it, and read it enthusiastically.
- Before the intro: close the doors, stop the music, and ask everyone to sit down.
- IF you do not have an Assistant, you can do it yourself, since you have already "warmed up the crowd" by greeting and chatting with them as they entered.

The following is a suggestion for how to begin. Please don't read it, just use it as a template for your own words:

- Thank them for signing Release forms.
- Ask everyone to look at the GROUP AGREEMENT template. (If you can project it on a wall or screen, do that now.)
- Explain the need for such an agreement, because we are creating a shared space for learning.

**GROUP AGREEMENT**—We all need to agree that:

- We will kindly support each other in all ways including safety.
- We will not critically judge ourselves or anyone else.
- We will risk looking silly.

- We will approach the work with enthusiasm.
- We will all participate, whenever asked.
- We will refrain from inappropriate touching.
- We will put away our mobile devices and keep them off until the breaks, which we will take approximately every 90 minutes.
- We agree to stay engaged in the work, be on time, and stay for the duration.
- We agree to keep the activities of this class confidential: what happens in class stays in class. (Please don't share specifics, as we have all agreed to be vulnerable and risk looking silly.)
- Ask if there are any questions about the Group Agreement? (Answer questions.)

Here's an example of what I might say to begin (edit at will!):

**Facilitator:** Everybody ready to begin? (They nod, etc.)

Great. So, if you accept the *Group Agreement*, I want to hear you speak up now and say YES! (They say yes.)

OK, great!

Now, you all just agreed to risk looking silly and approach the work with enthusiasm, so I want everybody to try it again. Let's *stand up, say yes, and show some enthusiasm!*

(They do so.) Much better! Thank you! Have a seat.

Now, we also just agreed that we will participate whenever we are asked. That includes sometimes, when we'll have a demonstration, and I'll need the help of a volunteer.

How do you feel about volunteering? (Silence or grumbles) I get it. Most of us don't want to be a guinea pig.

Still, you are *leaders*, and you have just agreed to participate when asked, and you have just agreed to do so with *enthusiasm*.

So now, I'm going to ask you to raise your hand if you will volunteer to join me up here in front, for the first demo of the day? (Hands go up.)

OK, I'll pick YOU! (choose one person) (Person moves to the front of the room.) Please tell us, what is your name?

(My name is _____.)

Excellent. Thank you for volunteering, _____.

Everyone, aren't you glad _____ volunteered, so you don't have to? Let's practice how we're going to support each other, individually, by thanking _____ for volunteering.

Let's *enthusiastically* thank _____ ! (They applaud.)

OK, _____, how does that make you feel, _____?

(_____ answers.)

That's good, but I think we can do better!

Everybody let's show _____ how much you *really* appreciate _____ for volunteering!

Let's give _____ a standing ovation! (They all stand and applaud.)

_____, how do you feel now? (_____ answers.)

Excellent! Thank you, _____. Here's a little token of thanks for being the FIRST volunteer of the day, _____. (Give some small gift.)

Thanks again, _____, you can have a seat.

Let's make _____ feel appreciated on the way back to her chair.

(They applaud.)

So, now that we know how we're going to enthusiastically treat EVERY volunteer, let's make a circle over here ... (all move to a standing circle) so we can get to know each other's names.

## Physical and Mental Warm-Ups

(Groups form a circle with ~12 to 18 inches between each person.)

**Facilitator:** There is a reason we don't wear name tags here. We want to eradicate any titles or other barriers to relationship building and learn to be observant. Also, we want to exercise what we call our *memory muscle*. (For those of you who already know each other, do your best to keep an open mind.)

As actors, the first thing we're taught is to *always* warm up our bodies and our voices.

The science about the connection between our physical, mental, and even spiritual parts is clear; if you sit around all day and don't move around, you suffer in all three areas.

The corticosteroids that cause fight, flight, or freeze response are released anytime when we're in an uncertain situation, like being in a new group. When we warm up and release those happy hormones that make us feel good about ourselves, we unleash spontaneous adaptability and problem-solving as a result!

This is why, as actors, we are taught to never go onstage, even for a rehearsal, if we haven't physically warmed up.

In fact, we usually do these as a group. So, let's take a few moments and warm up. If you have any problems standing up, you can do these exercises sitting down.

Note: Physical warm-ups are *not* optional.


### Exercise 2a—Stretching Warm-Up Exercises

- Perform some simple stretches and then …
- Give yourself a round of applause!


### Exercise 2b—Vocal Warm-Up Exercises

- Complete some gentle vocal warm-up exercises.
- Have everyone walk randomly around the room and repeat a tongue twister, for example, "unique New York, New York, unique."
- Reverse direction and repeat a different tongue twister.


### Exercise 2c—Mental Warm-Up Exercises

Everyone, come together and form a circle.

Now that we're warmed up physically, we need to warm up mentally.

Before we go any further, we need to practice what happens when we make a mistake. In improv, we view mistakes as *gifts*. Since we've ALL agreed that we'll risk looking silly, when you think you made a mistake, I want to hear you say something like, "I messed up! I goofed! I made a mistake! I took a risk! I failed!"

What I DON'T want to hear ANYONE say is a derogatory phrase, like "I'm so stupid!" or ANYTHING like that, OK? (No self-flagellation.)

So, let's practice.

Let me hear how you react when you make a mistake. … NOW! (They all shout out.)

Excellent!

When somebody else admits they made a mistake, we're going to SUPPORT that person!

And how do we do that? YES! We hoot n' holler and applaud!

Why do we do that? Because we're fallible. We make mistakes all the time.

OK, I know—you're thinking, "I work very hard to NOT make mistakes! If I do, I want to FIX it. Bad things happen when people make mistakes!"

That's true, but these are *exercises*. This is NOT reality. We are building relationships by showing vulnerability and telling the truth, as we see it.

More on that, later.

For now, I want you to randomly walk around the room as we did before, and practice saying, "I messed up!" or any of those kinds of phrases—whatever you want—and be enthusiastic!

When you get within range of somebody, make eye contact and CELEBRATE your goofs! YES! Mistakes are GIFTS in improv! They cause us to think in a different direction!

Let's go!

(They do.)

After a while, call them back to the circle. Now ask them to take a *different* place in the circle.

### Exercise 2d—Alliteration Name Game

This game is simple. There are only a couple of rules. The object is to practice Principle 1, accept all offers, to concentrate, and learn everyone's name.

I'll start and we'll go around the circle to the LEFT. Here's how it's played:

- Each person says an alliteration that begins with the same letter as their name (e.g., Curious Carol) and add a *gesture*.
- The next person begins *at the beginning*, with the first person's alliteration—name, and gesture, then adds their own.
- Play continues around the circle.

- The game ends when we've completed the circle … and we know everyone's name!
- To be fair, the facilitator will start and end the game.

Remember, whenever anyone goofs, we'll ALL support them … and if they don't realize they goofed, we're here to remind them by CELEBRATING their goof! After all, it's a gift! We'll thank them!

- Play begins and repeats around the circle until the end when the facilitator repeats everyone's name and gesture.

Everyone, give yourself a round of applause!
Facilitator invites everyone to sit down and take pen/paper.

## Debrief

- How did that feel? Comments?
- What surprised you about that exercise?

(Take a few minutes to field random comments, reinforce, and repeat common themes and aha-moments.)

## Exercise 2e—Truth Telling Game

(Note: This game is so popular, you will need a defined time to STOP the play. That time will vary, depending on the number of players and interest, e.g., a group of 20 may easily take 15 to 30 minutes. You decide.)

This game is played in a circle with chairs.

Direct everyone to bring a chair and make a circle. The facilitator stands in the center to explain and begin the game.

Facilitator: Now that we've learned each other's names, this game is designed to help us get to know each other a bit more.

This game is a little like musical chairs … with a twist … and may require you to move quickly.

If you have any movement issues, we have already all agreed, we will support you, so no one will be left out.

## Directions

- The person in the center begins with a truth about themself. (e.g., I have gotten a traffic ticket …)
- As soon as the speaker finishes the sentence, IF and only IF, that is also true for you, change seats! (The person in the center also looks for a seat.)
- Whoever is without a seat after the shuffle is "The Truth Teller" and must stand in the middle and begin the next round.
- Remember, whatever happens in the workshop stays in the workshop!

## *Debrief*

- What did you like about this game?
- How did this game impact your relationship with the group?
- Take five minutes and journal your thoughts about these two games and your experience here so far.

## *Can We Talk?*

It takes some time to prep a space for new construction, or just to add a new coat of paint. Likewise, it takes some time to prep a group for applied improvisational exercises.

Although it may seem more expedient to short-change this section, please do NOT cut into this preparation. (I named it *Crucial Beginnings* for a reason.) Based on my many years of studying the craft of improv, I am convinced that astute facilitators are deliberate about figuratively *setting the stage*, for the BEST learning experience. (The opposite is also true.)

Now, you and your group are physically and mentally prepped and ready to begin the work in earnest. Take a few moments to jot down your thoughts and questions before we continue. (You'll find space for your notes after each chapter.)

(Note: An example of a template for your Organizational Release Form/Liability Disclaimer is found in the Appendices. Use your own or add your logo and edit at will. Please assign an overseer to assure all agreements are signed before beginning of the workshops. Recall that if your employees are to earn continuing education for these hours, unless your organization has continuing education provider status, those permits needs to be coordinated well in advance.)

# Notes

# CHAPTER THREE

# Essential Improv Gear

*Strong people don't put others down ... They lift them up.*
—Michael P. Watson

***Principle 3: Avoid Yes/No questions.***
***Principle 4: Be helpful.***

## Avoid Questions?

Last year, when I moved into a new-to-me house, there was a lot of work to be done. I hired a contractor who showed up with a very large truck and an impressive collection of toolboxes and gizmos that filled most of the truck bed. I noticed he had a tool belt with the implements he used most often. As a nurse, that made sense to me; most nurses carry essential tools for the shift with the staples of patient care, for example, pens, tape, saline flushes, and ammonia pellets.

Although you may not be able to wear your tools on your belt, as a business leader, you also have specific tools you use every day.

As we begin building this new culture, the improv principles are our tools.

The directive to not ask questions may sound a bit counterintuitive. Notice, it says avoid *Yes/No questions.*

The reason is that although we always remind students to say "Yes, and ..." instead of "Yes, but ..." to move the action along, a Yes/No question will stop the action just as quick.

If our goal is to building relationships, we want to keep the conversation flowing *and be changed.*

Here's an example of the effectual conversation stall that occurs with a polar-based question.

Two participants stand side-by-side. The audience suggestion: a subway station.

**Player A**: You hear it's gonna snow today?
**Player B:** Yep.
**Player A**: How about them Raiders?
**Player B:** Yep.
**Player A**: You into soccer?
**Player B:** Some. You?
**Player A**: Some.

(BIG yawn.) Bor-ing! This scene goes nowhere.

The improv students are remembering Principle 1, the "A" of the A-C-E, *accept the offer*, but ... since they agree on everything, it's just *small talk*. The conversation goes nowhere because there is no C&E! There's no continuation and no embellishment. Neither player is helped in any way, there's no common problem, or conflict, nada. They have not even established a relationship, so we cannot be invested in the scene.

When people are checking their phones or reading a paper (you remember those?), they are essentially saying, "Don't interrupt me." They remain, each in their own little world. Don't let this happen to you onstage OR in real life!

IF more information was needed to create a relationship, a problem, or a conflict, a simple fix would be to ask open-ended questions, which would lead to interaction of some sort.

There's that word again: *relationship*. Let's explore that for a minute.

## Building Business Relationships

As humans, we care about creating *relationships*. Matter of fact, we care about relationships so *much*, that we will go to great lengths to read a story or continue to watch a TV show to *vicariously* experience a relationship with imaginary people we don't even know!

In real life, there's a saying that people like to do business with those they know, like, and trust ... but how do you get to know, like, and trust someone if they take directives from you? How do you tear down cultural walls and build bridges within the hierarchy, while maintaining the company org chart?

As leaders, such business relationships can get complicated.

Let's start with a glimpse of how a company culture might appear to some employees, at worst.

Imagine working at a place where you didn't have any friends. What if no one said hello or asked about your vacation, your family, your interests? What would it feel like, if you went through your day talking about the weather, but no one asked about *you*?

What would it feel like, if you were away for a few days (or a week, or a month), and when you returned, no one asked about you? No one asked how you were doing?

What if no one acknowledged your birthday?

What if no one noticed when you completed your work well? (You only got reprimanded when you slowed down, veered from policy, or made a mistake?) What if no one noticed when you went out of your way to help a teammate ... no one showed they cared, and so on.

These are examples of how any siloed culture can be a really sad place to work.

That's not only sad, but those circumstances promote the definition of social isolation, which is also a quick ride to employee disengagement, depression, burnout ... and worse.

If we practice the improv principles, we will grow business relationships and the workplace will be a much better place to spend your day.

In improv, we look for things we have in common to move along the scene, which simultaneously will move along the relationship onstage ... and offstage, the same principle applies.

You might both like baseball or it could mean you're both stuck in an elevator. It could be anything that gives you a reason to get to know each other and/or help each other.

In business, teams are assigned a project and must function as a team. If you are in a risk-averse industry where you are dealing with keeping people safe and/or saving lives, you may be required to lean on your training and function as a team rather quickly.

In either case, you sort out who will be in charge, settle on the various roles and tasks, and you're ready to do the work, whatever that might be.

Bruce Tuckman called this the four stages of group development: *Form, Storm, Norm, and Perform.*[1] Indeed, this process is repeated in every professional organization, in order to face challenges, find solutions, and deliver results.

## Make Your Partner Look Good

What happens when we apply the improv principles of avoiding questions and being helpful? One of my early improv faculty was Kat Koppett, who mentions the improv mantra, "Make your partner look good," or *be a blessing* to someone else.[2]

*Blessing?* You may ask: *Why is being helpful and making your partner look good a blessing?*

Because onstage, as in life, if your kind words make a situation easy, you will not only manage to complete the task and solve the immediate problem, but chances are you and your teammates will also feel good about each other, especially if the situation was scary or dangerous. (Interesting how that Golden Rule applies, eh?)

Likewise, in improv, the *help* you offer could be to accept a scene where you're close to death! Your *work* learning the improv principles is to just go with it and see what happens; a solution will likely occur in a way no one would have predicted.

That's the beauty of the applied improv exercises. If you keep an open mind and see what happens, you will be surprised, in a good way. To reiterate the A-C-E model, you *accept* all offers, *continue* (by adding info or asking open-ended questions), and then you help the scene progress by *embellishing* the action with a new fact, a secret, some history, an emotion, a new location, and so on. The possibilities are infinite!

This is because in life, as in improv, you rarely get the luxury of selecting your co-worker, your scene partner, or the situation. Nevertheless, in all cases, you do get to choose how to *respond* to the person and the situation with whom you are forced to interact.

Let's replay that scene at the beginning of this chapter and see what happens when we apply improv Principles 3 and 4, avoiding Yes/No questions and being helpful:

We'll use the same suggestion: a subway station.

**Player A:**  Hey, what's that dude doing?

**Player B:**  Eww. He's getting sick on the tracks!

**Player A:**  What's that?

**Player A:**  It's puke!

**Player B:**  Uh-ohhhh. The wind! The wind is whipping it this way! Watch out!

**Both:**  Augh!!!

What do you think? Do you see the difference? The second example has so many potential directions they could explore. Now they have a common problem! (Yuk, they both have vomit flying toward them!) How interesting! The players can spontaneously adapt to the situation, and we see infinite possibilities of how this scene could go, how their relationship might develop.

Of course, we could have played the scene differently.

We could have had Person A run and save Person C from jumping onto the tracks ... Then, Person B might have screamed, shouted, and threw a fit, or called the police, or gone to help ... Who knows?

There are as many variations as there are ideas. How might these principles look in your business? Here's an example.

Audience suggestion: A meeting room in a software company.

**Manager:** Good morning. Have you been reading your company e-mails? As of today, you'll need to clock out within 10 minutes of the time you are slated to work, per the schedule. Also, there will no longer be any overtime. Thanks for your attention.

(Turns around) Oh, and there's a new program we'll be using, starting today. Everyone needs to go through and sign off on the training. It's a revision, so it should only take you an hour. If you have questions, call IT.

(Employees look at each other, confused.)

**Sam:**  Wait! My team has a big project due Friday. We don't have all the info from a vendor on the coast yet and he says he can't get it to us until Friday morning, west-coast time. That means we don't have it til noon here, and we'll still need to add it to all the estimates and the prospectus for the client. The three of us already knew

|           | we'd be working over on, Friday, just to get it in on time. Now what? |
|-----------|----------------------------------------------------------------------|
| **Manager:** | You're clever. Work together. Figure it out. |
| **Sandra:** | Excuse me! If we only know about the project we're working on, and the stats are in late, how can we help another team? They'll waste time just trying to explain it all … and as a numbers person, if I calculate it wrong, that's my neck? We don't have a clue about their projects. |
| **Sam:** | There's gotta be some wiggle-room for OT when it's not our fault, IF the company wants to be compliant with the agreement and get it done by Friday … |
| **Manager:** | Administration has decided that, according to accounting, this is the most efficient way to get projects in on time and stop bleeding the company with overtime. |

(Looks at clock) Whoops. I have a meeting. If you have questions, e-mail me.

This is an example of a typical manager speaking to their team. The conversation is fictional. Even so, it is an amalgamation of several conversations you may have heard. I know I have!

Notwithstanding the difficulties of being the manager (the messenger), these types of conversations are concerning because of the obvious authoritarian and autocratic leadership displayed. The manager avoids the principle of being helpful by transactional terms. (It's also demeaning.)

In improv, this person is *blocking* the action by negating every possible statement of concern. She is also *blocking* any personal relationship with her team. (She is also taking advantage of her role with *status play*, which will be explained in depth in Chapter Six).

If we were to rewind this scene and play it in an improv workshop, utilizing improv Principle 3, it might go something like this:

|           | |
|-----------|---|
| **Manager:** | Good morning! It's so good to see you all. As you know, from the e-mails the administration has been sending out, today is the first day we rollout our new program of *project advancement*. We had a staff meeting about this last week where lots of your concerns |

were brought forward. I appreciate your thoughtful questions and possible solutions.

Oh, and there's a new program we'll be using, starting today. Everyone needs to go through and sign off on the training. It's a revision, so it should only take you an hour ... we hope! (Laughter) If you have questions, we'll have an IT supervisor going around to show you the new codes and help you.

**Sandra:** It was good to know that you don't expect every project to come in without overtime.

**Manager:** That's true. We have to use our common sense here. As many of you said, some projects can't be done according to original client agreement, through no fault of our own. The solution is that if you foresee that situation, or even when it's dropped in your lap late, call up to Risk Management and let the attorneys handle it. They already have language in place to cover you and they can ok the overtime you need ... within reason, of course. I hear chocolate helps. (gentle laughter)

**Sam:** Or a bottle of Grey Goose?

**Manager:** *I didn't hear that!* (general laughter)

**Sandra:** What about giving us overtime to learn the new software? I'm slammed today!

**Manager:** Thanks for bringing that up, Sandra. I am sending out an e-mail about that today. Everybody knows it's not possible to add educational updates plus do *everything else* and be out on time. Don't we all wish it were! (Nods of agreement.)

That's why the IT guys will be roaming around. They should be able to cut your learning time. They'll be here all week, and sign you off, so let them help you fit in the time.

Okay, I have a meeting, but I'll check back in an hour. I'll be around taking notes so I can hear your feedback on how it's going. Other questions, feel free to e-mail me or leave a message on my phone.

Either my assistant, Carol, or I will get back to you within 24 hours. And if you're off the next day, leave me your cell number and I'll text you.

How's that for *transformational* instead of *transactional*? Does that sound like a better place to work?

This is an example of transformational leadership or *managing by walking around*.[3] In the world of improv, this is the epitome of being helpful. The manager is open to ideas and willing to adapt to situations. That willingness to be helpful creates positive relationships and is a key takeaway in improv.

Now, it's your turn to practice the four principles we've learned so far: accept, risk looking silly, avoid Yes/No questions, and be helpful.

## Low-Risk Group Exercises

### Exercise 3a—Sound Ball

Facilitator: Everyone, let's stand in a circle.

Let's count off by twos, starting HERE. (… 1—2—1—2—etc.)

Everybody has a number, right?

Ok, I want all the ONES to take a step forward. (They do.)

When I tell you, I want all you ONES to find a completely different place in the circle.

Ready? GO! (They move.)

Now, reintroduce yourself to the person on either side. (They do.)

We are going to toss around an imaginary ball.

The rules of this game are simple:

FIRST, you start by making eye contact with someone else.

Next, you send an imaginary ball to that person.

You create a SOUND that sends the ball over. (Example: *Whooosh.*)

If you are the person receiving the ball, you must RECEIVE the ball with the SAME sound that was sent to you.

Let's try that. (Pick a person) _____, you make eye contact with ME and send me a ball with a sound. (Leader receives it, mimicking the sound.)

After I receive it, I will make eye contact with a different person and send the ball with a NEW sound. That person receives the ball with the same sound and sends it off with a different sound. Concentrate and keep your eye on the ball!

Got it? If you mess up, we will briefly CELEBRATE and keep moving on.

Let's practice it slowly at first and then we'll speed up.

Remember: The goal is to practice saying WHATEVER sound comes to mind FIRST.

Do NOT judge it, just let it drop out of your mouth. It takes concentration.

ALSO, if/when you mess up, we'll all CELEBRATE (for a moment), and then continue the game.

The game is over when the facilitator raises their hand and says, "Here."

Whoever has the ball at that time will pass the ball to the facilitator.

## Debrief

1. What surprised you about this game?
2. What was going through your mind as you threw the ball?
3. Were you judging yourself?
4. What happened when you slowed down?
5. What happened when you sped up?

## Exercise 3b—The Gift

Ask for a volunteer. Demonstrate one time, for the group.

## Directions

1. This game is played in pairs. Decide who will start. That person is the Gift-giver and the other receives the gift.
2. The Gift-giver turns away from their partner and thinks of a gift to give their partner.
3. The Gift-giver turns around, mimes carrying their gift (large, small, etc.) and presents it to the Receiver.
4. The Gift-giver must present the gift with a few words, but they may NOT tell the Recipient anything about the gift (e.g., "Happy Birthday, sister!")

5. The Recipient must "see" the gift as the *first thing* that comes to mind. (Don't let your inner critic judge this choice!) You'll receive it graciously, unwrap it, and comment on why you like and appreciate this gift. (REPEAT: Do not listen to the Inner Editor!)

6. The Gift-giver accepts the offer and builds on the story. Have fun with it.

7. Continue back and forth for a few sentences, then SWITCH.

8. Allow pairs to have enough time to be the Gift-giver at least twice.

9. At the end of the exercise, remind players to thank their partner.

### Debrief

- Depending on the size of the group, ask several pairs to share what was "given" and what the Gift-giver thought they were giving before the Recipient "saw" something completely different.

- Allow players to share their aha-moments.

Now that the group has had an opportunity to practice avoiding questions and focusing on being helpful, that's like adding a tool to our toolbelt. Let's see how we can progress from here!

# Notes

# CHAPTER FOUR

# Bravery Versus Cowardice

*Don't let the fear of striking out hold you back.*

—Babe Ruth

*Principle 5: Silence the Inner Editor.*
*Principle 6: Be adventurous!*

## That Little Voice Inside

This book didn't come easy.

I thought,

> There are loads of leadership books out there. Who needs another? After all, I didn't create an international brand. I'm not a CEO of a multi-million-dollar company. I've been a manager and I'm an entrepreneur with a team, but I'm not famous. Why would anybody want to listen to me?

That thought had nothing to do with the fact that I have many years of training and practice in facilitating and coaching leadership teams in applied improv, but that didn't seem to matter to the nagging voice. That little voice inside my head was whispering all kinds of cowardly things: "It's too hard to do; I can't write it. I *shouldn't write* it; I just won't do it."

I recalled the drudgery of the last book I wrote, the thesis before that, the missed social activities, the rewrites, the tedious hours slumped over a hot computer, the decisions, the *agony!* Why bother?

Why, indeed. Whenever we face a challenge, we seem to be tempted to have second thoughts (alternate facts?!) spring to mind.

Does this kind of self-talk sound familiar?

Of course, it does.

The fifth principle is a reminder to *Silence the Inner Editor*, but it isn't always easy.

You may recognize that voice, whispering in your ear, *anytime* you attempt something new. It doesn't matter what the *new* action is; that little voice is sure the *something new* will turn out to be *dangerous, stupid, foolish, trite, beneath your dignity, above your pay grade* ... whatever.

In improv and in life, when we try something new, we need to break away from the nagging feeling of dread. Judy Carter, in her book, *Stand-Up Comedy, the Book*, names hers, Slash.[1] I've dubbed mine, Cowardly Candy.

Have you named your Inner Editor?

Try it! You could name it anything that helps remind you to squelch that negative voice.

We *all* deal with this; some of us more than others.

That fear of failure makes us rethink the *cost of trying*.

Listening to your *Inner Editor* will urge you to set low expectations, since the fear of failure and inevitable embarrassment is just too much to bear.

The result? Many times, you talk yourself out of trying anything at all; you stay in the safe zone ... and stagnate.

This fear of failure is also linked to what psychologists call, *the imposter syndrome*. Even if we know we have some skill or expertise in any given subject, we second-guess our ability to take a bold step and try something new.

Do you recognize these lines from the Inner Editor's script?

- "Why should I even apply for that new position?"
- "What if that new co-worker who seems friendly is really a *frenemy*?"
- "What if my first date with this new person turns out awful?"

Worse yet, if you don't take care of yourself and your habits, this imposter syndrome problem can quickly spiral into real depression. (Note: *syndrome* is defined as a variable group of symptoms.)

What to do?

I suggest you talk to your Inner Editor like it was a little child. Tell it to go take a time-out, lie down and relax, take a nap, anything, but don't let it win the argument.

More good news: The by-product of improv training is that, afterward, the Inner Editor is stifled to the extent of allowing for more spontaneous and creative problem-solving. Now, that's something to celebrate personally as well as professionally!

### Risky Business

Principle 6 is to be adventurous. When we study applied improv, we *suspend our disbelief* about reality to train in emotional and social intelligence skills.

How does that work?

If you are a parent, you will recall how your toddlers struggled, learning to walk. Those first steps are always the most difficult. When the child topples over, do we say to them, "No more walking for you!" Of course not. We support their efforts enthusiastically. We shout and clap our hands, "That's it! You can do it! Try again!"

Similarly, in this improv training, we make a big deal out of taking risks, especially if we receive the *gift* of messing up! When we take a risk and then botch it in front of others, the natural reaction is to put our tail between our legs and hide, sulk, or sit on the bench ... but in improv, if we can recognize the mistake as a *gift and* incorporate the "gifted" idea into our play, we become emboldened to be (dare I say it?) an Adventurer ... and go where we haven't gone before!

This compliments and builds upon our positive attitude Principle 1, "Yes, and ...," which trusts the universe to reveal a new idea, and *Bingo!* You will be amazed at the degree of spontaneity this element adds to your life and the lives of those around you. In business, it is like the grease in the wheel, the gas in the car, the salt in the soup ... (OK, I'll stop with the similes. You can add your own here.)

Just remember that the Inner Editor will fight for your mental turf the rest of your life ... IF you haven't practiced subduing it.

The risk of Principle 6 in this training is that you're going to be asked to set aside the cautious mindset and adopt the improv mindset. The idea is, *if you leap, a net will appear.* That work requires that you practice Principle 5 and not judge yourself along the way.

Make room for the new awareness in your life as you practice these principles.

## Low-Risk Group Exercises

A method to assist you to shut-down the Inner Editor's annoying voice is to preemptively forgive yourself, knowing that as the games require more skill, you will risk being imperfect, each time. Yes, you will mess up, so decide to enjoy the process, and have fun with it!

When I present keynotes on the topic, I mention the findings of cognitive behaviorists (back to Piaget, Bloom, et al., and others). Beginning with the studies of children, then adults, they have shown that the best way to learn a new skill is to introduce an element of play. I call this the "Mary Poppins School of Improv." That is, when you find an element of fun, then, SNAP! The job's a game!

Here's an exercise to help the group relax, find some fun, and bypass the Inner Editor. Play it after other icebreakers.

### Exercise 4a—Freeze Tag—Round One

This game has many forms. We'll explore two of them. The first is very simple. (Demonstrate the first form with two volunteers.)

**Facilitator:** The object of this game is to practice silencing the Inner Editor and practice being adventurous. In Round One, it's a purely physical game; there are no words. Each person enters the scene and completes a picture. It's a fast-paced game that shouldn't take but an eyeblink for each "picture" to be completed.

To keep the action moving, you must silence your Inner Editor and act on the FIRST thing that comes to mind, in order to complete the picture. As soon as you take a pose, "freeze."

To demonstrate, we'll do this exercise in slow motion.

### Directions

1. Everyone stand in a circle with volunteer 1 in the middle.
2. Ask volunteer 1 to strike a pose—and freeze.
3. Instruct volunteer 2 to *complete the picture.* (They both will be frozen.)
4. Instruct the group to CLAP ONCE when they see the completed picture.

5. The CLAP is the signal for volunteer 1 to say, "Thank you!" and step away.
6. Volunteer 2 keeps their frozen pose, and facilitator steps in to create a new "picture."
7. The group CLAPS again when they see the picture.

Encourage the participants to ignore the Inner Editor and go with the first idea that comes to mind. The "CLAP and change" should happen quickly. No overthinking!

(Note: If you have a group larger than 20, consider two smaller circles.)

Beginning with the first volunteer, instruct the players to take turns in the center, going around the circle, clockwise.* Play for several minutes. Congratulate yourselves when everyone has had a turn.

*An advanced version of this game is to ask volunteers to jump in whenever they want. It's riskier, but also fun. (The caveat is that shy beginners may feel incapable of making the decision of when to jump in and play, so only do this with folks who have played the game before.)

### Debrief

- Explain how that made you feel? Why?
- Were you able to silence the Inner Editor? Why or why not?
- What delighted you about that exercise?
- What thoughts came up that "blocked" you from being adventurous?

### Exercise 4b—Freeze Tag—Round Two

### Directions

1. Now that you have the idea of physical Freeze Tag, we're going to up the ante.
2. Everyone counts off by 4s or 5s. Facilitator sends each of the 1s (etc.) to a different space.
3. They form in various areas of the room and make small circles.
4. Game begins with one person in each group (a volunteer or other directive) taking a pose.

5. Go around the circle. When the second person jumps in, they must justify their physical choice with one short sentence or an open-ended question.

6. Just like Round One, when the sentence is complete, the others CLAP to signal to person 1 to leave the scene and make way for the next person to jump in and justify their position.

7. Keep going around for several minutes.

Remember, don't prethink! Block your Inner Editor; just say whatever tumbles out of your mouth.

## Debrief

- How did that feel?
- Were you able to keep up the pace or did you find yourself overthinking?
- What happened when/if you found yourself prethinking how you planned to react?
- What happened when you jumped in without prethinking?

## Exercise 4c—Three Things

Here's another exercise to bypass the Inner Editor and concentrate on *play*. It's called Three Things. You will need to risk making mistakes and looking silly.

## Directions

Players *quickly* say whatever comes to mind and DO NOT *prethink*.

1. This game can be done in pairs, but it's most fun if completed in a group of four or five.
2. Facilitator instructs everyone to count off and form new groups of four or five in each part of the room.
3. Select the group closest to the front of the room to demonstrate.
4. The group chooses someone to start the first round.

5. That person names a category of THINGS, such as fruit, vegetables, famous singers, whatever.

6. As quickly as possible, the next person on the right says the first word that comes to mind, hopefully something in the given category.

7. Player to the right adds another THING in that category.

8. After three THINGS have been named, all clap three times while saying, "THREE THINGS, YAY!"

The next round continues with whoever stands beside the person who finished the first round (the person who said the last THING).

Allow players to go through several rounds before you call time. Remind players to thank their group before they take their seats. Round One example with a group of 5:

**Player** 1: FRUIT!
**Player** 2: Banana!
**Player** 3: Orange!
**Player** 4: Kiwi!
**Everyone** (clap three times with the words): THREE THINGS, YAY!

Round Two example:

**Player** 5: Vegetables!
**Player** 1: Potato!
**Player** 2: Squash!
**Player** 3: Hound dog!
**Everyone** (clap three times with the words): THREE THINGS, YAY!

Notice that hound dog was NOT a vegetable? That was a mistake, but NO MATTER.

Whatever *goof* was said is a *gift*. Celebrate the *goof gift*. (The laughter keeps the game going.) The idea is to say whatever comes to mind first and BLOCK the Inner editor.

The game continues, as the last speaker points to a new person to begin the next round.

Keep going for several minutes. The facilitator walks around and encourages the groups to quicken the pace for some real brain-fry fun!

Remember, don't overthink!

## Debrief

- What happened in your group?
- Share about what came up for you during that exercise?
- Were you surprised what popped out of your mouth?
- What delighted you about this exercise?
- Did you catch yourself trying to prethink during this exercise?
- What made it easy/hard for you?

Take a few minutes and write some notes in your journal about the last three games—Freeze Tag 1 and 2, and Three Things. (Allow up to five minutes.)

## Exercise 4d—Da-Do-Run-Run Game (Easy Rhyming and Audience Interaction)

Invite everyone to take a seat, then ask for four volunteers to come forward.

(Encourage the group as they enthusiastically support the volunteers.)

## Direction

Facilitator: We're going to continue practicing how to silence the Inner Editor by playing a rhyming game. Remember to do your best to rhyme, and above all, say WHATEVER comes out of your mouth first and be adventurous.

1. Ask the four volunteers to form a line.
2. Facilitator sings a sample first line, "I met him/her on a Wednesday and my heart stood still."
3. Practice refrain with the audience: (All participants sing) *Da-Do-Run-Run-Run, Da-Do-Run-Run.*

4. Players take turns, left to right. The next player sings the next line, rhyming the last word of the first line, after which the audience sings the refrain. (Ex: His eyes were blue and his name was Bill, *Da-Do-Run-Run-Run, Da-Do-Run-Run.*)

5. Next player sings the bridge—three lines, all rhyming the first line (Ex: Yah, his name was Bill, Yah! He owned a still; Yah, he was a pill! *Da-Do-Run-Run-Run, Da-Do-Run-Run.*)

IF anyone messes up, we'll CELEBRATE, and the game continues.

When this group is finished, practice thanking them again (and reward them with whatever imaginary or real prize you like ... (A dinner for two of lobster and champagne—*on Mars!*)

Now that the game has been demonstrated, play this again with another volunteer group or in a circle (if group is smaller).

### Debrief

- As a player, what was the struggle with your Inner Editor like?
- As a player, what surprised you most about this game?
- As a player, what were your takeaways?
- As the audience, what were your thoughts?
- As the audience, what delighted you about this game?

Before debriefing, take a few moments for everyone to make notes about their reaction to the exercises. Then, proceed with the debriefing.

# Notes

# CHAPTER FIVE

# Workplace Obstacles

*Attitude is contagious ... Is your worth catching?*
—Charles Schultz

**Principle 7: Be thankful; you have what you need.**

## Attitude and behavior

Next, we explore the improv mindset regarding an *attitude of gratitude*, how it relates to the *tear down walls and build bridges* concept, and the behaviors that can negate it.

Both in improv and the real world, your individual perspective is what all leaders and teams need to continue to adapt to fresh challenges. Commit to the applied improvisational exercises with the obvious challenge and settle into your own skin, for what you add to the work, just as you are. (Understand, there's no need to worry that you are not a skilled actor to do this work.)

True, in improv, you will often play another character who is totally *un*like yourself, just for fun, and to practice flexible thinking. Since there is no makeup, costume, or prescripted lines, just bringing *you* into the scene will result in authentic work. *YOU* are enough.

For example, the principle allows you to not worry if you need to confront a giant or a monster in your scene. In this world, you are enough AND you have what you need! Working this way in the imaginary world has direct relationship to the building of real-world adaptability and self-confidence.

In the business world, as leaders, we may have opportunities to meet and establish new relationships, however fleeting, with people every day. How do you feel when you meet new people, whether clients or colleagues? Are you (or some people who work with you) more of an introvert, who considers this a challenge? Might meeting new people be like facing a giant or a scary monster to you? To your employees?

An added benefit of improv work is that it allows you opportunities to change your limiting beliefs about the work of being a leader ... or a successful teammate. The determining factor, according to neuroscientists, philosophers, and poets alike, is that your *attitude* determines your success.

Reflecting back to Principle 1 (*accept all offers*), the principle of *gratitude* is inherent in the acceptance idea.

In practice, the *attitude of gratitude* is a foundational ingredient to what you might call a conundrum: the *anticipatory reaction* to whatever life has to offer. It may sound simplistic, but the research bears it out. If you think and act positively, that stance attracts positive interactions.

We can't hedge against all of life's problems, but science shows us that a thankful attitude not only ensures a better quality of life but also gives added years.

When we work with someone who listens and acknowledges what we say, feel, or think, our brain reacts with a rush of serotonin, and we feel a sense of rapport. We experience a sense of mutual confidence from this kind of relationship. We feel energized, our words flow, and we are drawn toward that person. We intuitively know, "We can work together."

In terms of how this attitude of gratitude work assists your teams to work together, let's elaborate on the concept of "Yes, and ..." in terms of self-confidence and the sequelae.

You and your teams can accomplish the A-C-E method, if you remember to practice arriving in the scene (without an agenda) and think to yourself, "I am enough and I have what I need."

Knowing you only have one task (acceptance) and that you are innately gifted with whatever tools, friends, powers, or objects you need, helps build the self-confidence needed to actively listen with an open mind and bring your authentic, best self into any relationship. This will have several positive outcomes, as we discussed.

In Chapter Three, we introduced the idea of what happens when we do *not* accept or *block* what has been given. Here's an example of two people whose conversation *seems like* they are accepting each other's ideas.

Audience suggestion: Two friends plan a vacation

**Player A:** Let's go on a cruise to Hawaii!

**Player B:** Yes! I've always wanted to go there, but I get sun-sick.

**Player A:** Oh, they have 50 SPF now! You should be okay.

**Player B:** Yes, but I'm afraid of boats; I get seasick.

**Player A:** Well, they have medicine for that now, too!

**Player B:** Oh, I hate to take pills ...

You'll notice that even when a person doesn't say, "No!" directly, the "Yes, but ..." answer is effectively the same as a "No." Furthermore, how do you *feel* when someone adds the "... but" to the "Yes?" You likely have a rather negative *attitude* about that person. We know that when we feel negativity of any sort, it causes an internal corticosteroid rush that effectively repels conversation, action, and of course, teamwork and/or friendship.

In improv, the action *must* go forward or it *stalls*. When the action does *not* go forward, it's likely because one person arrived in the scene with a personal agenda.

Here's a scene with two teammates discussing a new client project:

**Player A:** OK, looks like we'll be working together on this new project. What's the client's name again?

**Player B:** Malarky; Shamus Malarky. He just purchased a diamond mine.

**Player A:** Yes, I see, and we are the lucky team to help get the deed processed by proofreading this contract. We'll make sure all the I's are dotted and the T's crossed!

**Player B:** Yes, indeed-y. Get it?

**Player A:** Got it. So, how about if you take the first 10 pages, I'll take the next 10, and vice versa until we've gone through them all?

**Player B:** Sounds good. Maybe we can sneak our names onto the list of beneficiaries?!

(Oh, too bad we had to cut it off there. That sounds like the beginning of an intriguing story!)

If you read closely, not every response was an actual "Yes, and ..." statement. Nonetheless, each *offer* (thought) was accepted and built upon, so the action moves forward.

Universally, when we have our ideas accepted, we naturally feel *heard*. If you practice this simple exercise in real life, you will be well on your way to creating a positive relationship with others, as well as giving better customer service and client care.

Going deeper into the improv concept, the principle is that if/when we accept offers, whenever we feel stuck, remember that it's all just imaginary and *we have what we need*.

Yes! You can do *anything* in improv, *because you have what you need*. How cool is that?!

If necessary, you can pull an imaginary rabbit out of an imaginary hat to find the solution to the imaginary problem you face in the scene. You can build a castle, fly overhead, score the winning point ... Anything is possible!

The benefit of this practice to real-life situations is perhaps not so obvious. The practice of solving problems spontaneously and creatively in an experiential exercise is cleverly implanted in your subconscious. It's like the old saying: *You can't un-ring a bell.* When we practice these skills in improv, the brain stores the memory of a positive reaction to a creative and spontaneous solution.

When we assume we have what we need in real-life leadership and/or managing, we arrive with a positive attitude that we will be able to find what we need to accomplish a certain objective, and if we can't find what we think we need, we'll find another, better way. This *mind shift* allows you to practice being spontaneous and creative in your own life situations. As a result, you will become more proficient at solving all kinds of problems. It's a win/win!

## Driving Off-Road

In improv, *driving* is a behavior that looks like the opposite of *acceptance* and an *attitude of gratitude*, but it's a little different than blocking or negating. Instead, the *driver* leads the conversation and exerts their power over someone else. They bring their own agenda.

Do you know any *drivers*?

As a leader, do you feel it's your job to *be the driver*?

In improv, playing with someone who demands to *drive* the conversation is rather like playing with a spoiled child. Those participants are perceived as petulant, difficult, and no-fun to play with, because they insist on having their own way. They miss out on the magic that happens when they finally *let go* and allow other players to take a scene to a totally unexpected new direction.

Notice how, in a real-life hierarchy, everyone focuses on the leader. When doors are closed and employees are the last to know about big decisions, it creates workplace silos and a culture of semisecrecy. Since people are curious, gossip seems to ooze under the doors. It permeates everywhere.

In improv, *no one* is the leader of a scene, regardless of if they take on the character of a *dictator.*

In improv, *drivers* insist on the attention. It's what someone might say, when they have one idea and force it on another person, no matter what the context.

Here's an example:

**Player A:** (*Smiling*) Good morning, what a lovely day! Makes me feel like dancing!

**Player B:** (*Driving by not accepting the offer.*) My car broke down.

**Player A:** (*Trying to accept that offer and make sense of that comment*) Oh, sorry about that! Here, I'll take a look at it!

**Player B:** (*Driving and blocking*) My favorite color is blue, and Cousin Larry was a widow.

**Player A:** (*Trying to make sense of that comment and move the scene forward*) Ah, Larry. I remember him. He danced at your daughter's wedding!

You can imagine how frustrating it was for Player A in that scene. It seemed as if Player B was intentionally trying to be obtuse and/or bring attention to themself. In either case, they effectively derailed the scene.

Remember, the object is to focus on your partner and *make your partner look good. Driving and blocking puts* your partner on the defensive.

Think of your improv players as teammates, then think of the audience observer. Since the previous conversation is so unfocused and confusing, it would be difficult to follow. It would also be difficult to find a reason to be interested in this scene!

You can also see how Player A had to work really hard to make sense out of the random remarks of Player B. Instead of *accepting* and *building* on what the partner offers, Player B is *driving* with lines that seem to be an attempt to force the conversation off the road, so to speak. Player B has not said anything to deepen or explain the situation, the relationship, or to move the action forward.

Player A does a great job of justifying the offers of Player B, but the scene hasn't really gone anywhere; it's boring. Because of that, the conversation has a halting quality, the scene doesn't flow, the action is stalled. In fact, the worst part about playing with a *driver* is that it's no fun! (Note: Watching it is no fun for the audience, either.)

As leaders, when we come together to discuss a new policy idea, a project, and so on, we have a built-in focus. We assume we will be able to recognize the other person, understand, objectively evaluate, accept their comments, and realize some plan of action to solve the problem posed. We also must evaluate that person's words and actions *subjectively*, to be able to accomplish those goals. Sometimes our teammates can act like *drivers* in the conversation.

Here's how it might happen at work:

**Player A:** (*Smiling*) Hi there, it's my turn for Friday snacks; I brought blueberry muffins today!

**Player B:** (*Negating the offer and driving*) I don't like blueberries.

**Player A:** (*Accepting the offer and continuing*) Oh, I'm sorry to hear that. What will you bring on your Friday snack day?

**Player B:** (*Driving*) I don't have time to think about it now.

**Player A:** Okay, well, what I can do to help?

**Player B:** (*Driving*) Just let me get my coffee.

You'll notice that when someone purposely derails a conversation, the communication and connection are lost. There's no sure way back on track. Not only does the action stall but the other person also tends to wonder if the *driver* is in their right mind or just a *bleepity-bleep* negative person!

Both onstage and in real life, if you veer too far afield, your listener gets distracted, you lose connection and the point of your activity, and work stops.

In improv, this can quickly morph into the dreaded *crazy card*. Playing the *crazy card* is easy to do and is known in improv as beginner technique. You can see that when the scene gets so random, the story thread is never established, so it has no point.

I've seen this most commonly when teaching the very young or those who want to look smart or cool. (Note: It's neither.)

## Low-Risk Group Exercises

### Exercise 5a—Nonverbal Mirroring

(NOTE: You will need access to some varied music selections.)

Time: 10 to 15 minutes, depending on the number of partner switches. An easy, fun exercise to practice *acceptance* and an *attitude of gratitude*. This game has no dialogue. Players work in silence, while facilitator plays various sorts of music. (Vary the music every 20 to 30 seconds.) The goal is to work as *one* person.

Hint: Warn players not to go too fast or their partner won't be able to follow. This isn't a competition. Give players permission to stare at their partner's face.

### Directions

1. Find a partner you haven't played with before.
2. Partners face each other standing a few feet apart.
3. Choose who leads first.
4. The game begins when the music starts. Players must face each other and keep eyes locked.
5. Player A leads; Player B copies (mirrors) Player A's movements.
6. After about 30 seconds, the facilitator signals a change by shouting, "SWITCH" or sounding a bell, and so on.
7. Player B leads; Player A copies (mirrors) Player B's movements.
8. Continue changing leaders for several minutes (facilitator will vary the time).
9. Thank your partner.
10. Switch partners and play the game again!

Allow the exercise to continue for a few rounds. Remind players to focus on their partner, and *move as one person, looking in a mirror.*

## Debrief

- What surprised you in this exercise?
- What did you learn about nonverbal communication?
- How did this exercise cause you to feel differently about your partner(s)?

### Exercise 5b—Word-at-a-Time Partners

Time: 10 to 15 minutes, depending on the number of rounds.

## Directions

1. Find a partner you haven't played with before.
2. Partners face each other standing a few feet apart.
3. Choose who leads first.
4. The object is to say one word at a time and create complete sentences that make sense and are grammatically correct.
5. Facilitator assigns the *How to* topic, for example, *How to make a chili dog.*
6. Players take turns, adding only one word at a time.

Remind players to focus on their partner and concentrate on making sense. Allow the exercise to continue for a few minutes, until everyone has finished.

If desired, facilitator might suggest changing partners for a Round Two with a different (simple) *How to* topic.

## Debrief

- How many partners found a new way to make X (whatever it was)?
- What did you need to do to make answers work?

- How many were thinking of an idea while your partner had another?
- Was it hard to let go of your idea to accept your partners word?
- How often does this happen in the real world?
- What are your takeaways from this exercise?

After debriefing, allow a few minutes for participants to make notes about their takeaways from this section and these exercises.

# Notes

# CHAPTER SIX

# Heads Up

## Read Signals to Avoid a Crash

*In silence and in movement, you can show the reflection of people.*
—Marcel Marceau

**Principle 8: Actions speak louder than words.**

### The Actor's Toolbox

Clearly, nonverbal communication is an ancient practice, useful in so many ways, especially for groups who do not share a common language.

As a young girl, I recall meeting my nonhearing aunt and cousins for the first time. I noticed that although I didn't know sign language, we communicated well with mime and drawing pictures. Those experiences were in mind as I trained as an actor, learning how to establish a relationship with the other actors onstage by focusing on the other person, instead of worrying about my lines.

In my keynotes and workshops, I speak about what I affectionately call, "The Actor's Toolbox." Of course, one of these tools is nonverbal communication. The skill of reading body language and of using specific gestures to express meaning to an audience is critical.

Why is it that contemporary hearing adults often ignore the non-lexical material we all consciously or unconsciously provide? So often, we rush to judge others in the first few seconds and may misinterpret nonverbal signals.

When you take time to study these nonverbal behaviors more closely in applied improv classes, you benefit from renewed awareness of the possible meanings attached. This study is a tool to help you succeed in communicating more effectively.

Practice, as you go about your day and week when you are out and about. Do some people-watching. Make it a point to observe body language, based on:

- Their general posture when at rest.
- Their posture when talking on the phone, to a teammate, to a stranger, and so on.
- Their gait and way of walking.
- The distance they keep between others when speaking.
- Their facial expressions at rest, and with various emotional reactions.
- Their arm and leg positions standing and sitting.
- Their hand motions.
- Their types of touching.

Next, in real life or onstage, when you enter an area where you will engage with others, even if the scene unfolds as though you are two strangers, take a moment. Breathe. Look before you speak. What do you see? What information is each person telegraphing? How does their body language make you react?

- Does the person invade your personal space or keep a far distance?
- Do they slump or stand upright?
- Are their arms crossed?
- Do they have hands on hips?
- Do arms hang limply to their sides?
- Do they clasp their hands, twist their fingers, or hide them behind their back?
- Does this person look you straight in the eye or gaze at the ceiling or floor?
- Eyes open or narrowed?
- Mouth held tight or relaxed? Smiling? Frowning?
- Eyebrows high? Low? Furrowed?
- Does the person reach out to shake your hand? Is the handshake vigorous or limp? Lengthy or curt?

- Do they pat your back? Touch your shoulder? Poke your chest? Avoid touching?

Recall that the other person is reading your body language, too. What message are you sending?

### Status Play

Actions also belie feelings of position, or (in improv) what we call, *status*. It is the combination of nonverbal behaviors and socialized types of speech. To understand these behaviors and how they are incorporated into relational behaviors is another "tool" in The Actor's Toolbox. This helps us understand how to increase relational communication by neutralizing *status play.*

We all are familiar with schoolyard bullies, who scheme to embarrass or distance themselves from perceived uncool kids. They have certain ways they walk and talk that broadcasts their *high status*. Similarly, the uncool kids display their lack of, or *low status*, with different gaits and vernacular.

For example, in the following scene, the actors were told to play *low status versus high status.*

The audience suggestion: A donut shop

**Customer:** Can I get a dozen glazed donuts, please?

**Shopkeeper:** A dozen glazed? You have your nerve! Who do you think you are, asking for glazed when you can see we only have powdered donuts and maple bars!

**Customer:** Oh? Uh, sorry, I didn't know ... I thought you have glazed donuts all the time.

**Shopkeeper:** You and your assumptions! How dare you come into my shop and demand glazed donuts! It's FRIDAY! Don't you see the sign? Glazed donuts are GONE by noon on Friday!

**Customer:** Uh, no, I didn't see the sign. This is my first time in here.

**Shopkeeper:** I see! You didn't even take a number!

**Customer:**     Okay (takes number) ... it says 37 ... I don't understand, I'm the only one here.

**Shopkeeper:**  Well, well! I suppose you think you're FIRST! Just because you don't see anyone here, doesn't mean I'm not busy! I have a STACK of orders to fulfill here on the desk. They all have a number. They came in virtually. Yours is *37*. Get in line!

**Customer:**     Thanks; I can see you're busy. Maybe if I can help, I'll get some donuts—any kind—by 6 p.m. when my wife gets home. Donuts are her favorite and if I can't get glazed, I'll take whatever. I don't want to disappoint her; she doesn't like to be disappointed.

**Shopkeeper:**  Well, alright! it took you long enough! How else do you suppose I could handle all this work! Get over here and start filling these orders. And make it snappy!

**Customer:**     Yessir. Anything else, sir?

**Shopkeeper:**  YES! Call me when you've finished. I need a break! (Leaves.)

**Customer:**     (works furiously ...)

Silly? Yes, and ... we find the conversation funny, because of the reversal of what are the usual customer–shopkeeper roles. Did you notice that although the players were in contention, they were also moving the scene along by using the A-C-E principle?

The delight of the learning in applied improv is that we get to play fantastical scenes where people mess up and/or die and nobody really gets hurt. In fact, in the mind of the audience, the messier it gets, the funnier it's likely to become!

In real life, especially in the corporate world, and certainly in government work, you recognize, people play status games all the time. Do not assume that learning applied improv means your group will go around holding hands and singing Kumbaya all day. (Sadly, not.) Forewarned is forearmed, as the saying goes. You will use this knowledge to understand and subtly deflect the office status games, so you can have a rational conversation without wrecking your professional relationships.

How might the awareness of *status* help you to turn the tide and balance a conflict?

In the United States, and in most western countries, we have a personal desire to stand out as rugged individualists.

Indeed, most parents encourage individualism and do their best to inculcate a drive for success in their children. We give ourselves permission to go against the grain, as it were, to get what we want and achieve anything we can dream. At the same time, by nature, we are social animals. Given a social hierarchy, we tend to follow what the leader does and emanate the group behavior.

C-Suite leaders learn that they must lead, since they have (presumably) advanced education, a title and leadership position, and *the buck* stops with them. Employees learn that they must play the submissive role for the same reasons. Therefore, blame for miscommunication in the workplace has been passed largely to leaders.

A case in point was made in a recent documentary about the culture change that happened after aerospace companies Boeing and McDonnel Douglas combined.[1] Unfortunately, the merger and acquisition process ultimately created a dangerously unsafe workplace culture in a risk-averse industry. A 2022 documentary film with testimonials from employees included accusations that, after the merger, people didn't want to point out any problems to management, because the employee would immediately be blamed for it.

Especially in high-stakes industries, this is a huge problem.

You are striving for a balanced workplace culture, where employees feel free to offer suggestions and know they are heard, so that your organization will grow and be better, so that everyone will benefit. What could you do to encourage employees to speak up?

Assertiveness training programs exist for this very reason. We must ask: Are such programs helpful?

Based on countless research articles of the past 40 years, the actual effectiveness of assertiveness training on behaviors is up for grabs. To teach assertiveness through role-playing sounds good, but there is an important caveat attached to this work. When teammates have a strained working relationship, there is no sense of safety, or *trust,* for the one in the subdominant role to *speak up.* Open communication is hampered, for fear of repercussions, despite the training.

Happily, improv training is based on the premise that relationships build trust, trust creates a sense of safety, and safety creates a culture where everyone has a voice and right to be heard.

In your organization, if you are an effective leader, you strive to be open to new ideas, include everyone, be positive, learn people's names. What can you do to create those behaviors in others?

Based on her study of Piaget's cognitive behavioral psychology, Viola Spolin, originator of the improv method, was the first educator to posit that these relational, culture-changing abilities are skills that can be learned.[2] The unusual premise she proposed was that as adults, no matter what age, in order to lose the fear of recrimination or embarrassment, we need to learn to *play* again, without socialized fears.

As a result, she constructed a classroom environment where students learned it was *safe*:

- Safe to risk being incorrect.
- Safe to feel silly.
- Safe to laugh at your foibles.
- No shame, no blame, for imperfection.

Spolin also recognized another problem. To overcome existing internalized fears, you must establish a sense of *trust* between people who were often total strangers—or worse yet, already had some sort of antagonistic relationship outside of her classroom.

Thanks to her studies, the exercises Spolin introduced were results of the concept of scientific discovery about social behaviors, that is, she didn't propose a few rules and lay them down as a law. That brings us back to the concept of *status.* Spolin noticed that students automatically deferred to her or other faculty as leaders, who are paid to dispense wisdom and *orders.* She suggested that students should approach the work as experimentation. During her classes, she let the question, "What if ...?" guide the play.

That idea of scholarly, playful, inquiry is our goal. Within the applied improvisational exercises, we learn to play with this concept. It's as though we are working out at the gym, challenging ourselves and strengthening our improv-muscles, so to speak. In my many years of facilitating these workshops and classes, participants tell me that these *status games* are some of the most eye-opening exercises of all.

A typical first exercise is to help students learn how we intuitively react to others in unspoken context.

Accordingly, we do any number of physical exercises to *feel* how that plays out in our sense of status: Do we feel kingly walking slouched-over? Do we feel like a child if we twirl? How do we feel when we look another person straight in the eye? Or when we drop our eyes and avoid eye contact? We study movement and find the meaning or possible meaning in every nuance, then translate that to *status*.

My clients tell me that when we have a whole group in class for team building, it is remarkable how one or two-days' training can make such an impact on the culture of the office or clinic.

The opposite is also true.

Logically, if part of the group misses out on the training, the culture change takes longer. To reap the greatest rewards, in terms of creative and inclusive culture, decision makers should find a way to enable all team members to attend and to make sure new hires also have opportunity to experience the training.

In improv, if the faculty is skilled in coaching and debriefing, the rate of ROI is much higher than for many other required team-based programs. The reason is clear: improv is fun and kinesthetic. We know from Benjamin Bloom's Taxonomy of Educational Objectives that these active participatory and experiential methods create a safe environment so learning can take place.[3]

An interesting example of how *safe* environment creates a culture of trust that facilitates learning is filmmaker Michael Moore's film, *Where to Invade Next*.[4] Moore journeyed to Finland, home to some of the world's smartest students, for his documentary. He spoke with Finnish faculty and students, and learned that their educational system has little in common with the United States.

For example, Finnish students are *not* at school all day and are given little homework. They have no multiple-choice questions on exams, nor do they have standardized tests. (They must learn the material well enough to write about the subject from memory.)

A notable addition, in my view, is that Finnish school programs include many of the subjects that American schools have excluded, such as art, poetry, music, and *free time* to play.

Granted, Finland is a small country, about 5.5 million people, or somewhat smaller than the state of Minnesota, and about 2.2 million less than the greater San Francisco Bay area. Hence, the comparison is not an easy equivalency. And yet, these students, despite strict rules, focus on lessons made to encourage curiosity and creativity. They are nurtured and allowed to play. They rank high in IQ and have few discipline problems. Students call their teachers by their first names, and advanced students assist slower or younger students when their work is complete. They learn to read and speak other languages early and often.

That sounds like a recipe of safety, trust, and equal status, doesn't it?

What can we learn from the Finnish method of education that we can apply in organizations?

## Low-Risk Group Exercises

### Exercise 6a—Nonverbal Behaviors

Let's practice observing and internalizing nonverbal behaviors.

### Directions

1. Count off by twos; divide the class in half.
2. The 1s will play *high status:*
   - Ask this group to think WHO they are (what job/title) and what THOUGHTS are going through their mind as they interact with others in the room.
   - Based on that, ask them to walk and behave in the *high status* ways (e.g., erect posture, head high and still, stare, look down their noses at others, and so on.)

3. The 2s will play *low status:*
   - Ask this group to think WHO they are (what job/title) and what THOUGHTS are going through their mind as they interact with others in the room.
   - Based on that, ask them to walk and behave in the *low status* ways: slumping, shuffling, averting glances, and so on.
4. At the command, everyone moves randomly around the room, for about two to three minutes, making only *nonverbal* contact.
5. Facilitator states, "Switch!" and the 1s now play *low status*, the 2s play *high status*.

## Debrief

- How did it feel to play the *high-status* character?
- The *low-status* person?
- What will you remember from this exercise?

## Exercise 6b—Status Scene With Numbers

You will need a deck of cards for this exercise. Depending on the size of your group, you should select an even distribution of numbers, 1–10. You can add a few face cards and mention they are to be treated as 11s.

## Directions

1. Each participant takes a card and looks at the number for a few seconds, then puts it in a separate pile, or keeps it hidden.
2. Participants will have a few seconds to think of a character based on the number. Create a name, an occupation, and so on.
3. Participants will randomly walk around, in character, introduce themselves, and have conversations with one or two persons at a time.
4. Give a suggestion that they are reacting to the others in a common area (restaurant, etc.)
5. Facilitator signals "SWITCH" at 1 minute, and participants find a reason to move to a different person(s) and begin a new conversation.
6. Allow for at least three conversations, depending on the size of the group.

*Debrief*

- Ask participants to line up in the order of their card number, reveal their card, and explain about the character they created.
- Ask the group to name one thing that person did that revealed they were low or high status?
- How did it feel to play that status?
- What surprised you about this exercise?

### *Exercise 6c—Onstage Status Scene With Partners—Round One*

## Directions

1. Ask for two volunteers to demonstrate a scene with status-play.
2. Ask for a suggestion of a relationship between two family members (e.g., father/son).
3. Determine who plays which character.
4. Assign high status to one, low status to the other.
5. Ask for a situation (e.g., son arrives home late).
6. Ask for a location where these two people might meet (e.g., kitchen).
7. Tell the players you might do some "side-coaching" if they get stuck.

Facilitator: Allow the scene to play to a logical conclusion, with the high-status character keeping their high status, and so on.

(Note: If the players get bogged down in Yes/No question or *driving*, coach them to say the first thing that comes to mind *as that person*, remind them of their status, and see how the scene plays out. Beware of too much coaching that impedes the flow of ideas. Only interrupt if needed.)

*Debrief*

- Ask the players to stay onstage. Ask, "How did that feel?"
- Ask the audience what they noticed that showed subtle high or low status displayed.
- Discuss.

*Exercise 6d—Status Scene With Partners—Round Two*

## Directions

1. Ask the players to take the same suggestions and play the scene again.
2. Only now, slowly switch STATUS roles during the scene (e.g., Father becomes wimpy, son becomes controlling).

Facilitator: Allow the scene to play to a logical conclusion, with the characters swapping their status.

### Debrief

- Ask the players to stay onstage. Ask, "How did that feel?"
- Ask the audience what they noticed that showed subtle high or low status displayed and where they observed a transition to opposite status.
- Discuss what they learned from Round One and Round Two.

Ask the group to answer the following questions and write reflections in their journals:

- When might you see high- or low-status behavior? Explain.
- What are your takeaways from these exercises?

Invite participants to read out some of the key phrases that occurred to them during this journal reflection.

# Notes

# CHAPTER SEVEN

# Take Heed

*We have two ears and one mouth so we can listen twice as much as we speak.*

—Epictetus

***Principle 9: Look and listen to understand, not merely to respond.***

## Building Empathy

This principle builds upon the underlying assumption of relationship building. That is, empathy equals caring and curiosity. We must care enough to be curious about what and how another person presents ideas. That curiosity drives us to focus on the skill of active listening, which is the observation of nonverbal cues plus spoken words, with the object of *understanding*. Active listening is the key to creating and maintaining a trusting relationship.

You may argue that you are already aware of nonverbal cues and how words are spoken. You may notice these things subconsciously or you may notice them because you have a somatic reaction, for example, you feel flushed, your stomach ties up in a knot, you clench your jaw, or you burst out in laughter.

The difference here is *purposeful* noticing, which implies caring as opposed to merely reacting. When you look for nonverbal cues and listen to words for attitudes and meanings, you put ego aside and actively listen to understand more objectively. For example, notice the other person's vocal quality. Do they speak in hushed tones, loudly, or just right for normal conversation? What is the rhythm, cadence, or speed of their speech? How are they positioned? Arms across chest? Slouching? Eyes downcast? How do they hold their head? How do they walk into a room? Shake hands, and so on?

As business leaders, you are likely taught something about persuasive communication, or how to influence the buyer. Instead of logical arguments, we are going to dip into the Actor's Toolbox again to find other ways to build relationships and connect, so we communicate on another, less salesy, level.

We learned about nonverbal observation. We expand on that with the natural extension of that tool, *verbal mirroring*. This method is used to verify and acknowledge what was said, and to draw out the client's experiences and feelings. This skill requires active listening skills. In acting, this is a bulwark of how to be grounded in the reality of the moment and diminish the natural tendency to be thinking about our predetermined directives, when we combine the nonverbal observation with verbal mirroring. It's a very useful tool for all leaders to relax in the moment, really listen, and stop thinking about the schedule, the next meeting, the desire to end the conversation, whatever else is on your mind, for the moments you have the attention of another human.

(Note: In conflict, we purposely break any predetermined peaceful relationship by *verbally distancing*.)

Here's an example of verbal mirroring.

The suggestion, an office meeting:

**Employee:** He won't leave me alone.
**HR:** He won't leave you alone?
**Employee:** No! He keeps texting me day and night.
**HR:** Oh, he keeps texting you ...
**Employee:** Yes, I can't get anything done!
**HR:** You can't get anything done? Tell me more ...

Note: Although mirroring is most often very successful in helping build trust with a client, be careful how it is presented. This method can also be used as a tactic to intimidate, when done in a mimicking or taunting manner. (Refer back to those schoolyard bullies!)

### Recognize Inactive Listening

*Inactive* listening is another habit that stymies conversation. As a result, people lose focus and interrupt. This loss of focus is often a result of habit of egoism (blocking). Sometimes, people lose focus because they are easily distracted, for example, with childlike enthusiasm, or are immature or impatient. Generally speaking, an interruption acts as a conversation disruptor, because the other party never gets to finish a thought.

In the improv lectures and discussions, we assist players to *actively* listen and recognize when they lose focus and are tempted to interrupt. We show ways to get back on track, listen to each other, and spontaneously develop creative solutions to whatever problem, conflict, or quandary is created.

In the business world, there are many instances where someone will interrupt. An enthusiastic interrupter can fuel a deeper conversation, depending on your relationship. Active listening can help get the conversation back on track if the interrupter is recognized and the interruption validated. Commonly, once trust is reestablished, that leads to better understanding.

### The Unbroken Circle

Active listening that creates effective communication can be illustrated as a continuous circle. I picture it like a game of catch. One person sends a message, the other receives it *and* sends a message in return. It gets bounced back and forth. This is called *closed-loop* or *circular communication*. Note that the communication loop is necessary for partners and teams to work well together.

That said, there are also times that call for *open-looped* or *one-way communication*.[1] This is especially useful in times of emergency when life-saving instructions need to be given by one speaker and received by a helper or a whole team. For example, during a code blue, when first-responders shout, "CLEAR!" that is the time to jump back, not the time for conversation.

In business, most of the time, such open-looped conversations in daily communications are counterproductive.

Depending on the body language that accompanies such one-sided, open-loop conversation, various strong messages can be implicated by nonverbal responses (e.g., rolling the eyes, shaking the head, walking away, etc.). Indeed, the open-loop communication is one of the main reasons for inter- and intraprofessional *mis*communication. We all know what happens then ... mistakes, blame, shame, poor client service, and worse.

Businesses also need to *up their game*, in terms of learning to raise their Emotional Intelligence and Social Intelligence quotient. In improv, we work to accomplish those goals, plus one more: to increase our Creativity Quotient.

The following exercises will assist to practice active listening and increase emotional, social, and creativity quotients by learning to consider *both* verbal and nonverbal aspects of the behaviors of the other person.

## Low-Risk Group Exercises

### Exercise 7a—Interrupting

Let's explore this open-looped communication exercise.

The facilitator asks for a suggestion for a relationship that two people might have. The subject will be their family tree. (If players don't know their history, they may invent something.)

### Directions

1. Everyone, select a partner whom you don't know well.
2. Find a space where you can face each other about three feet apart.
3. Decide who will be A and who will be B.
4. Person A begins with this sentence, "My family came from ..."
5. Person B interrupts with a Yes/No question or a contradictory statement.
6. Go back and forth for about one minute, then switch roles.
7. Thank your partner.

The facilitator halts the exercise, asks everyone to find a new partner close by.

### Exercise 7b—Variation

This exercise is the same, only this time, Person B apologizes every time they interrupt.

1. **Player A** begins with this sentence, "My family came from …"
2. **Player B** interrupts and apologizes.
3. **Player A** continues.
4. **Player B** interrupts and apologizes.
5. Go back and forth for ~1 minute, then switch roles.

## Debrief

- How did you feel as the main speaker? The interrupter?
- Did the apology make any difference? Why or why not?

### Exercise 7c—Sportscaster Olympics

We'll practice closed-loop or circular communication with this exercise.

## Directions

1. Place three chairs in a row on the side of the stage, facing the audience.
2. Ask for five volunteers to join you onstage. Have them count off, 1 to 5.
3. Numbers 1-3-5 will sit in the chairs. They are the WIIFM radio Olympic sportscasters.
4. The two others are silent athletes in this scene; they begin by standing, center stage.
5. Instruct the sportscasters: Starting with 1, you will take turns, each stating one sentence, commenting about the action onstage. Each will accept, acknowledge, and build upon what the others have said, and the action you see.
6. Instruct the athletes: You begin after we receive the sporting event suggestion, warming up, and then competing in the event. They will pantomime action in SLOW MOTION.
7. Ask for a suggestion of a sport (e.g., golf).
8. Ask for a suggestion of a common household object (e.g., vase).
9. Explain that we are going to witness an obscure sporting event that has never been played, called _____ (e.g., vase golfing).

If there is time, select five other volunteers and play another round with a different sport.

## *Debrief*

- Ask the players, "What worked in that scene?" "What didn't work so well?"
- Ask the audience, "What did you notice about that scene, in terms of flexibility and listening?"
- Take a few minutes and journal your reflections on these three games.


### *Exercise 7d—Listening Game*

Ask for a volunteer to demonstrate this exercise.

This is another pair's mirroring exercise, to practice listening. Each partner will have one minute to explain an average event in their life (e.g., what I did to get ready this morning; my favorite meal; how I learned to shave; how to make a bed; and so on; or ask for a suggestion). Use a timer.


### Directions

1. Direct players to find a partner they haven't worked with yet.
2. Give each other permission to stare at each other's face and mouth.
3. Explain they will need to SPEAK SLOWLY.
4. Pairs decide who goes first, as the Storyteller.
5. When facilitator says "BEGIN!" the Storyteller has one minute to talk about the agreed-upon, average event.
6. Meanwhile, the Listener stands close enough to hear what the Storyteller is saying (without invading the teller's personal space) and focuses on each word the Storyteller speaks.
7. As the Storyteller speaks, the Listener gently, quietly "mirrors" each word. They will, in essence, be speaking together.

After one minute, call "SWITCH!"
At the end, call time and remind players to thank their partner.

*Debrief*

- How did that feel as the Storyteller? The Listener?
- Was it easy or difficult? Why?
- Share with your team and journal your reflections.

# Notes

# CHAPTER EIGHT

# Divergent Thinking

*Act now or forever miss the moment.*

—Candy Campbell

***Principle 10: Focus on your partner.***

## A Paradox

In cooking or in natural sciences, when we increase the temperature of a substance, moisture evaporates, and the resulting solution becomes concentrated or *reduced*. Onstage, when we concentrate our energy on our scene partner, extraneous distractions evaporate, and our attention is reduced to laser-like focus on the other person.

The paradox here is that this attention to detail triggers a flood of interest and creative energy around the other person. It's not as though we fall in love with the scene partner, since we might not really have much in common with them, offstage. The noticeable change is that when we concentrate, *really concentrate* on the essence of that person, who they are, how they are moving, what they are saying, they become *interesting* and new ideas are unleashed. It's as though, when we get *self* out of the way, a whole new shower of ideas comes cascading into our consciousness.

The concept of *divergent thinking* in improv is an extension of the idea to silence that Inner Editor (see Chapter Three), to believe in yourself, and build on your strengths, so you are able to give to your partners the attention they deserve.

In applied improv training, we concentrate on being *in the moment* when we share the stage with whoever happens to be present. Usually, we don't have the luxury of choosing who our partner onstage (or offstage) will be. (Isn't that just like life?)

So, the best way to accomplish this is to change our usual, inward focus on self, to others, and be open to hear different ideas and opinions. It doesn't mean we need to accept everything another person says or thinks. It means we become more open to real learning through communication, in terms of the old-fashioned definition of an educated person.

As a result, when we give our full attention to what the other person says or does, we pick up on cues, can respond with authenticity, and be adaptable. The benefit is, this practice increases the trust factor in a relationship, no matter your hierarchical position.

### Waffling in Improv and Life

In improv (or in real life), if you are unfocused, unsure if you have freedom to speak, or are anxious for any reason, you might opt to do nothing. You may feign action or do only as much as necessary to make it *appear* you are contributing, even when you're not. In real life, you may appear to be listening in order to make a quick exit when the person stops to take a breath! All of these motivations lead to the same outcome.

In improv, we call this *waffling*. When we waffle in a scene, it goes nowhere. When we waffle in life, we may miss an opportunity ... or get fired.

After all, if it's real or onstage, it's now or never. A*ct now or forever miss the moment.*[1]

True, you may not have what you *want*, but if you open your mind to the possibilities of what the universe has to offer, you may get what you need, despite what Mick Jagger sings in the background.

Here's an example from improv and then we'll look at a business situation.

**Player A:**  I heard bears hibernate in caves during the winter. Oh! There's a cave.

**Player B:**  Do you think there's a bear in there?

**Player A:**  I dunno, but I'm afraid of bears. You go see.

**Player B:**  Why me? You go first.

**Player A:**  ME? I went first last time we went on a hike.

**Player B:** You call that a hike? It was Black Friday at the mall. Go on, I'll cover for you.

**Player A:** Cover what? My dead body?

As you can see, there's some clever dialogue, but the audience is already getting bored. Why? The action is stalled. In improv class, whenever the action stalls, the facilitator will say, "Go into the cave!" (or wherever).

Here's a better example using several improv principles: Focus on your partner, be adventurous, and you have what you need.

**Player A:** I hear bears hibernate in caves during the winter. Oh! There's a cave.

**Player B:** (Grabs A's face): Do you think there's a bear in there?

**Player A:** (Breaking loose): I dunno. Let's find out!

**Player B:** Well, today my horoscope said: "You will face a challenge." Lucky for us, I have this telescopic repeating rifle in my parka, just in case.

**Player A:** Okay, here we go! Everything will be fine!

**Player B:** What could possibly go wrong? (They go into the cave).

**Player A:** Oh, look, a cute lil' bear sleeping!

**Player B:** Looks just like a puppy, all furry and soft. (petting it) Hello, lil' bear ...

**Player A:** Uh-oh, don't look now, but there's it's momma and she's ... waking up?

**Player B:** And she doesn't look happy!

**Both:** RUN!

In corporate life, it may look something like this:

**Player A:** Did you check your e-mail? We have a new policy.

**Player B:** What now?

**Player A:** You have to check e-mail within 24 hours or you get dinged.

**Player B:** I've been gone three days. How would I know?

**Player A:** I dunno. You probably got dinged.

**Player B:** That makes no sense. Has anybody talked to
management?

**Player A:** What for? Same ol' same ol'...

**Player B:** You're right ...

Ask yourself: When you have waffled, were you able to change the status quo?

Speaking up takes bravery. You know employees will grumble at times; it's human nature. But what would happen if your employees felt they worked in a place where their ideas were valued?

**Player A:** Did you check your e-mail? We have a new policy.

**Player B:** What now?

**Player A:** You have to check e-mail within 24 hours or you get dinged.

**Player B:** I've been gone three days. How would I know?

**Player A:** I dunno. You probably got dinged.

**Player B:** That makes no sense. Has anybody talked to management?

**Player A:** I thought about it, but ...

**Player B:** We have to speak up so the policy will be changed!

**Player A:** You're right.

**Player B:** Ok, let's go in there right now. It'll sound better if there are two of us.

**Player A:** Wait. Maybe we should write down some ideas—have an alternate proposal.

**Player B:** Good point. Let's do that and get some feedback.

**Player A:** And some other signatures!

## Nothing Comes From Nothing: Carve a New Path

A stall or a complaint only serves as a spotlight to solve a problem if we act as a *positive deviant*; that is, we create better ideas to solve a problem.

This presupposes a collective communal intelligence, which is also the bedrock of the political improv practiced by Augusto Boal. In this format, the audience has permission to stop, interrupt the scene, assume a character, and change the action.[2]

In such cases, Boal prepped the audience with exercises prior to the play to maintain order and understand the basic principles of civil discourse and improv. This can be a very powerful type of group game, since the whole audience feels welcome to add to the dialogue.

The solutions found in some of these civil improv performances have been cited as the basis for change in local communities.

With the following exercises, we will practice focusing on our partner(s) and taking action.

## Low-Risk Group Exercises

### Exercise 8a—One Word at a Time Introductions

These exercises will allow participants to focus on their partner and practice flexibility and spontaneity.

Ask for two volunteers to demonstrate the game onstage. Ask them to stand side-by-side, lock arms and speak as one person, each adding one word at a time. They must focus out and speak at a normal speed. (No looking at each other.) Facilitator asks a few questions to demonstrate.

Example:

| | |
|---|---|
| **Facilitator:** | Hi, who are you? |
| **Player A:** | Hi, |
| **Player B:** | my |
| **Player A:** | name |
| **Player B:** | is |
| **Player A:** | Emily |
| **Player B:** | Smith. |

### Directions

1. Find a partner who is approximately the same height as you.
2. As demonstrated, you will speak as one person, each saying one word at a time to make a sentence.

3. Stand side by side, lock arms, and find another pair to introduce yourself (as one person) and have a short conversation.
4. Keep moving around the room and introduce yourself to several groups and have short one-word-at-a-time conversations.

### Exercise 8b—Round Two—One Voice

Ask for two more volunteers to demonstrate the variation of this game onstage. Ask them to stand side-by-side, lock arms and speak as one person, simultaneously, with One Voice, and answer questions.

Example

**Facilitator:** Hi, who are you?
**Both:**      Hi, my name is … (etc.)

### Directions

1. Choose a new partner.
2. Stand side-by-side, lock arms, and have an introductory conversation with other pairs.
3. This time, you will speak, simultaneously, as one person. You must not allow one person to drive the conversation.
4. You will keep eyes focused out (not at each other) and speak at a normal pace as you move around the room.

### Debrief

- What was the most difficult for you? One-at-a-time sentences or One Voice?
- What made it easier?

### Exercise 8c—One Voice Expert

Put three chairs close together onstage, plus one to the side. Ask for three volunteers to take one of the three row seats. (Facilitator will act as commentator in the fourth seat.)

Ask for a suggestion of an unusual hobby. (This could be a combination of two suggestions, for example, a verb and noun, as in carving + banana = banana carving.)

The purpose of this exercise is to become the expert on _____ (the hobby).

The TV interview is a show where an expert author is interviewed about their new book and take audience questions.

## Directions

1. The expert must sit close together and face front at all times; players must not look at each other. Instruct the players to focus on each other and breathe deeply, in unison, three times, before they begin the exercise.

2. The expert must speak with one voice. Players must NOT allow one person to drive the conversation.

3. The interviewer opens the show and welcomes the guest, who is an expert in the suggested profession.

4. The interviewer asks the following questions: Expert's name, how long they have been studying, how they got started, and so on.

5. Allow audience participation. Ask for QA and allow the expert to answer a few questions.

6. Thank the expert and give a very generous (imaginary) prize as a thanks for coming on the show!

### Exercise 8d—It's Tuesday

Improviser and Theatresports founder Keith Johnstone calls this exercise *It's Tuesday*.[3]

The goal is to quelch *waffling* and force *action*, by employing active listening. It can be done with two or three players.

Ask for three volunteers to play this scene. Say it will require focus and good listening skills.

- Ask audience for suggestions of three distinct emotions.
- Ask for a suggestion of a place where these people might be.

- Ask for a suggestion of a relationship (brother–sister, girl-friends, co-workers, etc.)
- Ask for a suggestion of a profession for each of the players.

## Directions

Explain players will practice *overaccepting* and *building on the story thread* using exaggerated emotions that increase as the scene progresses.

1. Whatever is said, they must:
   a. accept it;
   b. justify the partner's words;
   c. overreact, using the assigned emotion;
   d. move the action forward;
   e. no waffling allowed!

(Hint: Most emotions can be categorized as glad, mad, sad, fearful, surprised, or disgusted. If the suggested emotion is "frustrated," coach the players that they can become *more* frustrated until they get angry or disgusted, whichever emotion has not been used.)

Give yourself permission to experiment! An opposite reaction can create great comedy.

## Debrief

- How did it feel to choose boldly?
- What happened in the scene that surprised or delighted you?
- What will you remember about this scene that might be useful in your life?

Share with your team and journal your reflections.

# Notes

# CHAPTER NINE

# Truth Serum

*Stories validate and reinforce your message and offer an outlet for thoughtful reflection.*

—Craig Harrison

**Principle 11: Follow the Story Spine and be changed.**
**Principle 12: Treat others like you want to be treated.**

## Storytelling in Life and Onstage

From the essence of time, before neuroscience was an established subcategory that explained how *what* we perceive is translated by our brains, people have loved a good story. It's a basic method that knits us together as individuals and groups. Take two strangers and one common experience and ... *Zap!* ... you get a *story*.

Stories contain the lived experience, the essence of human relationships. Good stories teach a lesson that verifies our solidarity as a group. It shows we care about each other and about positive outcomes. The story could be one with a happy ending, a funny ending, or a scary ending that acts as a warning. In either case, we tell stories for a reason.

Much has been written about the importance of storytelling in terms of learning and cognition. Indeed, our brains seem (nearly literally) *wired* to accept a story and make sense of the process it shepherds. Story leads to understanding, empathy, and memory.

Even babies seem to understand stories. This fact was brought home when I held my infant grandson, who watched his older brother play with two makeshift puppets. One puppet, a blue Teddy Bear, went along happily ("Lalalalala," sang the brother), and the other, a Tyrannosaurus Rex, attacked poor Teddy Bear. The baby wailed! Brother changed the scene. Mr. Dinosaur kissed the blue bear, and the baby laughed. All this was perceived at a mere seven months old.

As we get older, besides plain entertainment, a good story also helps establish credibility. We want to know the mission and vision of a company as an individual and see that it ties to their brand. We want to know *what they stand for* and *why they do what they do.* We want to know *their story.*

Author Simon Sinek defined this further. In a free market society, as producers of anything, we want to be viewed as authentic, so customers want to engage with us and purchase our products.[1] *Our story* helps establish a clientele. We want clients to know that they will be treated with respect, that they will be treated according to the Golden Rule.

As leaders, we want to be viewed as authentic so shareholders and stakeholders will feel relaxed enough to trust our work and live more productive lives. *Our story* helps establish a trusting relationship.

Your employees, no matter where they work, also want to be valued. They want to know that there is a work ethic of reciprocity. If they have no leadership title, they want to have *a good story* to establish their reputation as a team player.

If we do have a leadership title, we are expected to be a responsible individual who works to motivate others. In tense situations, *our story* establishes what we believe in and inspires others to follow our lead.

You may be thinking, "STOP. Not so fast. Some stories are just fiction! If a true, new story equals *news*, an untrue story equals *fake news.* Improv is make-believe, ergo, it's fake."

Am I saying you should learn to lie?

No.

Just as an athletic coach guides the team in *practice* drills and experimental moves, the improv coach guides players to *practice* improv story drills and *experiment* with new moves. With this type of deliberate practice, players and/or colleagues become more cohesive in the *real game of life.*

How?

The success of an *improv story game* depends upon our willingness to *suspend our disbelief* and trust the other players. Viola Spolin said the key was to *get out of your head* and keep the *Point of Concentration,* or focus, in mind.[2] That focus should always be the other person in the scene.

When we put our trust in others, when we force ourselves to block out everything else and focus on the other person, the effect is quite miraculous. With trust and focus, we find ourselves more *willing to be changed.* Almost as a reward for good behavior, a simple change in focus and attitude stimulates creativity and imagination to solve countless problems. When we seek not to interpret but to communicate, the work of storytelling is directly translatable to business real-life problems.

## The Practice of Imagination

In my many years as an actor, director, and improv facilitator, I have concluded that putting your imagination to work produces the most unlikely results. It never ceases to amaze me what happens in improv classes … *in a good way.* Students are continually surprised and delighted by what they and their classmates come up with. Certainly, these imaginative stories could come to life by no other means.

Unlike algorithmic plans for solving scientific problems or the insistence of some *suffering artists* who complain that they must be internally stimulated to entice the *Creative Muse,* the process of creativity in improv is more like gathering flowers than finding a cure for cancer. It should be more enjoyable and less depressing, because it invites spontaneity, adaptation, problem-solving, and team building. These outcomes are predictable results when participants share a common, albeit fictitious, lived experience. The mere experience forges relational bonds.

One of the reasons these creative exercises are so successful is because they are so much *fun*! Once students relax enough into the process and trust they will not be humiliated or blamed when they take a risk and things don't work out so well, they feel *free* to take risks, speak out, experiment, and problem-solve in new ways. Facilitators must be careful not to blame or shame, but gently side-coach students to *stay with the problem.*

In order to be successful, your coach will present what playwright Kenn Adams calls the *Story Spine* with its parameters, to give structure to your stories.[3] This should be familiar; it is the same as every bedtime story ever told. It is also the framework of almost every Hollywood film. Interesting that the story spine can be developed in so many genres and that it never gets old!

## Story Spine—Example

"Once upon a time," explains who the story is about and what usually happens.

- Harry, an attorney, and Sally, a law clerk, worked at the same office.
- They didn't really know each other, and they didn't particularly like what they did know about each other.

"And every day," explains the status quo:

- They barely talked when they worked together on a case:

**Sally:** See Mrs. Glen today about the robbery case?
**Harry:** Yep.
**Sally:** Get a statement?
**Harry:** Yep.
**Sally:** That's good.
**Harry:** Yep.
**Sally:** How many more depositions 'til we close?
**Harry:** Two more.
**Sally:** Okay.

"Until one day," explains the story's twist.

- The whole team was mandated to attend a weekend improv workshop.
- Like most of the team, neither Harry nor Sally wanted to give up their weekend, but they had no choice.

"And because of that," is another story twist.

- Harry and Sally had a conversation and got to know each other better. They learned they both like dirt bikes. And each other.

"And because of that," …

- Harry and Sally started a club for people who like dirt bike racing.

"And because of that," …

- Harry and Sally began riding dirt bikes together.

"Until finally," provides a pivotal moment.

- Harry and Sally got married.

"And ever since that day," is the bookend of the story.

- Harry and Sally ride their dirt bikes to the local theater on Improv night.

[Extra] "The moral of the story is," provides a moral or a callback comment:

- Be careful who you ignore at work, because he might be the dirt bike you marry.

## Low-Risk Group Exercises

### Exercise 9a—One-Word Sentence

Now let's practice active listening to understand, not just to respond, and create a story.

Participants take turns adding a word to make a sentence. Each person is allowed to add ONLY one word at a time, for two minutes.

### Directions

1. Everyone, select a different partner, one who has either the same shoe color or shoe size as you.
2. Find a space where you can face each other, about three feet apart.
3. Decide who will be A and who will be B.

4. **Player A** begins with one word.

5. **Player B** adds a word.

6. Keep going back and forth until a sentence is completed.

7. Take turns beginning a new sentence, until facilitator calls TIME.

The subject is "A day in the life ..." (or some suggested title).

### Exercise 9b—Story Spine

Find a partner or have the group sit in a circle. Get a suggestion for a place. Take turns adding to the narrative using the story spine framework.
Do it again!

### Exercise 9c—Limericks

As a variation, try creating a limerick! Here's the framework:

(rhyme A) There once was a man from Kent,

(rhyme A) Whose leg was unusually bent.

(rhyme B) He hobbled to church,

(rhyme B) Fell down with a lurch,

(rhyme A) The other leg now has a dent.

### Debrief

- How did that feel?
- What surprised or delighted you about these exercises?
- Write down your favorite limerick that was created today.
- Practice writing limericks when you are stuck in traffic or need to switch from left to right brain!
- Share with your team and journal your reflections.

# Notes

# CHAPTER TEN

# Building Your Next BARN

*The secret of change is to focus all of your energy not on fighting the old, but on building the new.*

—Socrates

## Step One—Check!

If you've waded through every chapter in this book, congratulations!

Why should that excite you? According to polling surveys by PEW Research in 2021, 23 percent of U.S. adults say they have not read even one book or a part of a book in the past 12 months![1]

That response included any sort of book, including e-books, audio books, and traditional paper-based books. (True, a telephone survey with 1,502 respondents will yield less than exact results, but you get the point; given the trend for hybrid in-person and virtual work situation and extra time at home for so many, it's equally shocking.)

So, kudos to you!

In case you are reading the last chapter first (confession: I do that, too!), let's summarize what this book covers. In our time together, you have learned to focus on the following communication principles:

1. Accept all communication offers, gracefully.
2. Limit questions unless they are necessary to the conversation.
3. Be of service to others.
4. Don't listen to negative self-talk.
5. Speak up, even though you risk looking silly or wrong.
6. You have what you need to successfully communicate.
7. Have a thankful attitude.
8. Observe actions.
9. Look and listen before you form a reply.
10. Give the other person your undivided attention.

11. Know what makes a good story.

12. Obey the golden rule.

Now it's your turn to spring into action! How will this knowledge play-out for you, in your organization?

**My promise to you: IF you practice these AIE principles, you will experience a catalyst reaction within your organization *and* in your personal life.** (No joke; it's not a laughing matter!)

So, how DO you weave these principles into the fabric of your life?

When you take these principles with you into your personal and professional life, you will experience the benefit of what we improv aficionados like to call, *The Improv Mind*, or as my friend Craig Harrison says, "Improvocation!" (Some add a metaphysical component, but we need not be so esoteric here.)

It may seem too good to be true, but it has been my experience, working with various groups, that when these principles are introduced early and often (e.g., improv "jams" or workshop tune-ups) to an organization, you will definitely see positive results in many ways.

Some previous clients state they have been tapped to leadership positions, perhaps because the *improv mindset* inspired newly expressed energy, enthusiasm, and innovative ideas. Some report that they feel more connected to even the contentious personalities in their family or at work. One fellow said, because of improv training, he practiced "Yes, and-ing …" principles with his girlfriend, focused more on her nonverbal cues, and felt such a new connection, he proposed!

You may not have as dramatic an epiphany, but most students of improv are enthusiastic about the method and want to share it with others, since the process and the learning is so effective … and fun! But how?

We know that to impact a particular culture and effect change in the habits of the person, it's important to establish an awareness of your product and differentiate it from all the others, which brings us to the next step.

## The Vision

Since you have the sense of urgency and recognize you want to change the culture, it will be helpful to understand the nuances and know what causes a culture shift on a larger scale.

Allow me to add a note about the assumptive definition of the word, *culture*. Generally, these are the social institutions that make up normative behaviors, for example, specific language, idioms, vocal intonations, foods, types of currency, and so on. These ways of knowing are taught from early years.

Some people believe that we can bring about a change in culture by just knowing about it; as though visiting a different country for a few days while on vacation and observing their differences would be enough to change us, personally, for a lifetime. It's possible, but unlikely.

True, it's quite another thing to actually move to a different country and be immersed in it. I've had the honor of living in five different countries and I can attest, with time, a foreigner has the distinct advantage of continued observations, sharing ideas, recognizing types of patterns, and comparing our old assumptions to the new experiences. Change is much more likely, then, because we have recognized a new model of possibility.

Indeed, the idea of university education is based on the idea of immersing oneself into random exposure to brilliant ideas and unfamiliar people. We send our young people to college to have those experiences and learn how to be open-minded.

However, is it not presumptive to think that the *understanding* of a behavior is the only catalyst for change? If knowledge were all that is needed, there would be no more overweight people, no anorexics, no smokers, no substance addicts ... or at least the numbers would be far fewer.

Think about it: As a leader, how often have you forced employees to attend or complete a learning course online, that was intended to improve your communication skills? If you're in a risk-averse industry, the answer is likely, *too often!*

And what is the result? How many times have you, in the C-Suite, or you, as the employee, completed a training and thought, "Okay, I've checked that box, things will be better, now."

Or have you spent tens of thousands of dollars on a particular "communication" program that essentially lectured to the group all day and promised results because they all got a book?

Have *any* of those (other) programs changed your work culture for the better?

Exactly. That's *not* how culture change happens.

## Sketch Out the Plan

So, what kind of learning can actually facilitate a *cultural shift*?

History shows us that only a few inventions have shifted the cultures of the world: the wheel, the printing press, the Internet, the cellphone … and that more abstract philosophies and events, such as religious orders, political movements, wars, and rituals can also cause cultural shifts. The common denominator is a sense of urgency (or need to have) and/or social pressure. Both require kinesthetic learning of some sort.

In his book, *Cumulative Advantage*, Mark Schaefer, talks about the how we build momentum of acceptance for any idea that might change the culture. He posits that our needs and expectations change when we experience a *crisis*.[2] That's when we are ready and *willing* to look for new opportunities and make a change.

Considering your latest organizational unrest or crisis (whatever that might be), might your organization need to un-silo groups and improve inter- and intraprofessional communication to improve creative problem-solving? Would that kind of change benefit your customer experience and satisfaction surveys?

Might better team communication decrease the number of in-fighting? Wouldn't it be better to retain employees by enacting a program that can help change the culture? If so, this may be the perfect time to consider a program to help *tear down walls and build bridges* (the name I give my workshops), within your organization.

## More Evidence That Deserves a Verdict

Scroll back a few years to the time I was working to complete my doctoral work. Academia prescribed that I finish a study, with pre- and postsurveys, regarding the process improvement I chose to undertake. I'm happy to report that the managers of the hospital where the research took place helped me choose two clinical teams who had evidently been *at loggerheads*. An inter- and intraprofessional group was assembled. It included nurses, nurse managers, a physician, respiratory therapist, and a social worker.

After a daylong workshop using applied experiential exercises at this renowned hospital, the participants gushed with glee about the skills they had received.

One quipped:

The best thing about today was that the method is fun, it's easy, and it's really applicable to any life situation. The worst part about today is that not everyone in our unit was in this class. What a difference it would make if they were!

That said it all. As a matter of fact, the desire to tear down those silos between teams has propelled my work for the past two decades. This passion to increase interprofessional communication and decrease miscommunication was the impetus to continue my studies and write a doctoral thesis on the subject.

Although applied improv training isn't new, it has been generally misunderstood as making silly jokes or performing off-the-cuff. (Thanks to TV improv shows that cut out any scenes that producers and sponsors consider *not funny* enough.) This is so untrue!

Improv professionals understand the principles outlined here perform at the top of their intelligence with inclusivity, grace, and humor. Applied improv training for practical use requires knowledgeable facilitation and training. Unfortunately, this sort of training has not been widely acknowledged for the powerful tool it is.

As we've seen, improvisational training assists participants to practice the principles that we all instinctively know but have not always adopted. Applied improv gives people the opportunity to help forge relationships with others whom they have, for a variety of reasons, avoided.

Remember this: Results don't lie. What you have been doing to solve the miscommunication problem hasn't worked.

### Your Next Step

So, what's a caring, helpful person to do? (You know you are intelligent, or you wouldn't be reading this book!) The good news is, you are being presented with both a *crisis* and an *opportunity*.

Having read this book, you can understand that the penultimate way to study improv is with a group. This may be an especially good time to consider an AIE program to rebuild your workplace culture from the top-down, inside out. You have my guarantee that your experience will be like the many groups I have taught over the years (including the Silicon Valley start-ups and the health care teams who couldn't get along), who hail the improv workshops as the BEST medicine to build up an ailing team.

How could you decide if you are ready to implement an innovative transformation and acculturation program with an improv professional?

Here's the summary of the results your team will experience, when you hire an *experienced improv facilitator*:

- Increased Emotional Intelligence;
- Better employee communication;
- Higher employee retention rate;
- More efficient teams;
- More productive workplace;
- Happier customers and clients;
- Reduced cost to hire and train new employees;
- Less HR litigation;
- More profit.

As you can see, everyone wins: Employees, customers, management, stockholders, and administrators. We all win!

Would it make sense for you to consider an applied improv leadership retreat, workshops, and/or train-the-trainer course? I guarantee they can be transformative for your corporate onboarding, for breaking down silos, establishing better connections, communication, and creativity in your organization.

You will be the hero when you bring in such a fun, transformative program to help change your culture to one of safety and caring for the individual employee as well as your client.

Thanks for playing along with me in this book two of the four-part series on *Improv to Improve ...*

Here's how to find me: https://candycampbell.com and candy@candycampbell.com

With kindness, Candy Campbell, DNP (and a lot of other letters you probably could care less about).

# Notes

# Appendix A

## Participant Organizational/Release of Liability Agreement Template

The undersigned participant of the **applied improvisational exercises classes** (e.g., *Tearing Down Walls and Building Bridges*) agrees to be responsible for their own conduct and actions during the class and releases (organization and facilitator names) from any claims and demands that may occur during participation in the class or from incidents or accidents, held at (location) on this/these following dates.

Furthermore, I agree to release (organization) and its employees from any liability, which may arise from incidents or accidents involving myself, while on class premises, to the extent allowed by law.

This release of liability form will be valid for the date(s) of the class(es), per registration agreement.

_____

NAME—Please PRINT

_____

Signature                                    Date

_____

(e-mail)                                      (mobile phone#)

# Appendix B

## Group Agreement

I understand that applied improvisational exercises classes involve group participation.

I agree to the following rules of engagement with the group:

- I will support my classmates, in all ways, including learning safely.
- I will not criticize or harm my classmates or myself.
- I will participate in class, whenever asked.
- I will risk looking silly.
- I will approach the work with enthusiasm.
- I will refrain from inappropriate touching.
- I agree to keep class activities confidential; what happens in class stays in class.

_____

**Signature**                                    **Date**

# Glossary

**Accept**—To accept an *offer* someone has given as though it is TRUE. (Ex: "You DO have lovely bat wings. How do you keep them tucked in when you swim?")

**Advance**—Add another item to move the scene forward once the initial offer is accepted. (Ex: "Congratulations! I heard you were elected Mayor!")

**Blocking**—To deny the offer with a response of "no" or ask a question that takes it off the table.

**Callback**—Mentioning an offer from earlier in the scene or from a previous scene. This connection tends to delight the audience. (see **Reincorporation**)

**Comment**—Speaking to the audience in an aside, aka: "breaking the fourth wall."

**Continue**—(see **Advance**)

**Driving**—Prethink or force your own ideas within a scene.

**Embellish**—Adding to an offer with a statement that gives the scene some hitherto unknown detail or history. (see **Advance**)

**Endowment**—Any offer that defines a person, place, or thing, for example, characterization, relationship, location, or emotion. (Ex: "Hi, Jane, when does your daughter go back to college?")

**Gagging**—Making a joke to make yourself look funny or cool, at the expense of the scene. (It's a practice to avoid.)

**Gibberish**—An invented language comprised of nonsense words and phrases.

**Gossiping**—Speaking about anything that doesn't pertain to the present moment, for example, introducing a new character or talking about a dead one. (Note: This is a tool that works well in long-form improv; it's an advanced technique.)

**Hedging**—(see **Waffling**)

**It's Tuesday**—Overacceptance of an offer. (A good warm-up exercise.)

**Mugging**—Making cartoonish faces instead of reacting truthfully. (It's a practice to avoid.)

**Objective**—The goal of the character(s) in a scene.

**Raise the Stakes**—(see **Advance**)

**Reincorporation**—(see **Callback**)

**Space Object**—Using pantomime to express real objects and actions.

**Status**—The perceived social position of a character that determines how they react to others, for example, high/medium/low status and may change throughout a scene.

**Talking Heads**—Refers to a static scene where no actions are taken. (Another practice to avoid.)

**Waffling**—Making nebulous offers or not committing to a specific action or reaction.

# Notes

## Chapter One

1. Psychology Today (2021).
2. Cameron (1992).
3. Industry Training Report (2021).
4. Cameron (1992).
5. FORBES (2021).
6. *Harvard Business Review* (2022).
7. Press Ganey (2021).
8. Gallup Podcast (2022).
9. Psychology Today (2021).
10. *Harvard Business Review* (2022).
11. Ciçek and Kılınç (2021), pp. 372–384.
12. Goleman (2005).
13. Lupien (2009), pp. 434–440.
14. Lupien, Juster, Raymond, and Marin (2018), pp. 91–105.
15. Anderson, Krathwohl, Airasian, Cruikshank, Mayer, Pintrich, Raths, and Wittrock (2000).
16. Csikszentmihalyi (2007).
17. Edwards (2012).

## Chapter Two

1. Alda (2018).
2. Rogers (2003).
3. Hall (2014).
4. Gallup (2022).
5. Tedone and Bruk-Lee (2022), pp. 289–304.

## Chapter Three

1. Tuckman (1965), pp. 384–399.
2. Koppett (2012).
3. Blanchard and Johnson (2016).

# Chapter Four

1. Carter (1989).

# Chapter Six

1. Kennedy (2022).
2. Spolin (1963).
3. Anderson, Krathwohl, Airasian, Cruikshank, Mayer, Pintrich, Raths, and Wittrock (2000).
4. Michael (2016).

# Chapter Seven

1. Bashir, Boudjit, and Zeadally (2022), pp. 78–86.

# Chapter Eight

1. Tolstory (1943).
2. Ibid.
3. Johnstone (1979).

# Chapter Nine

1. Sinek (2017).
2. Spolin (1963).
3. Adams (2007).

# Chapter Ten

1. PEW Research (2021).
2. Schaeffer (2021).

# References

Adams, K. 2007. *How to Improvise a Full-Length Play: The Art of Spontaneous Theater*. New York, NY: Allworth Press.

Alda, A. 2018. *If I Understood You, Would I Have This Look on My Face?: My Adventures in the Art and Science of Relating and Communicating*. New York, NY: Random House.

Anderson, L., D. Krathwohl, P. Airasian, K.A. Cruikshank, R.E. Mayer, P.R. Pintrich, J. Raths, and M.C. Wittrock. 2000. *Taxonomy for Learning, Teaching, and Assessing: A Revision of Bloom's Taxonomy of Educational Objectives*. London: Pearson.

Bashir, N., S. Boudjit, and S. Zeadally. 2022. *A Closed-Loop Control Architecture of UAV and WSN for Traffic Surveillance on Highways*, pp. 78–86. Computer Communications, vol. 190. https://doi.org/10.1016/j.comcom.2022.04.008 (retrieved April 24, 2022).

Blanchard, K. and S. Johnson. 2016. *The New One-Minute Manager*. New York, NY: Harper Collins.

Cameron, J. 1992. *The Artist's Way*. New York, NY: Random House.

Carter, J. 1989. *The Stand-Up Comedy: The Book*. New York City, NY: Dell Publishing.

Ciçek, B. and E. Kılınç. 2021. "Can Transformational Leadership Eliminate the Negativity of Technostress? Insights From the Logistic Industry." *BMIJJ* 9, no. 1, pp. 372–384. https://doi.org/10.15295/bmij.v9i1.1770 (retrieved February 27, 2022).

Csikszentmihalyi, M. 2007. *Finding Flow: The Psychology of Engagement With Everyday Life*. New York, NY: Hachette Book Group.

Edwards, B. 2012. *Drawing on the Right Side of the Brain*. New York City, NY: Penguin.

Forbes. July 28, 2021. www.forbes.com/sites/forbestechcouncil/2021/07/28/why-your-employees-are-leaving-en-masse-and-the-surprising-factor-that-will-keep-them/?sh=2cf2ff6e40fb (retrieved February 27, 2022).

Gallup podcast. February 11, 2022. www.gallup.com/cliftonstrengths/en/389552/great-resignation-is-really-great-discontent.aspx (retrieved February 13, 2022).

Gallup. 2022. *Clifton Strengthsfinder* website. www.gallup.com/cliftonstrengths/en/home.aspx (retrieved March 20, 2022).

Goleman, D. 2005. *Emotional Intelligence: Why It Can Matter More Than IQ*. New York, NY: Bantam Books.

Hall, W. 2014. *Improv Games*. San Francisco, CA: Fratelli Bologna.

*Harvard Business Review*. January 11, 2022. https://hbr.org/2022/01/11-trends -that-will-shape-work-in-2022-and-beyond (retrieved March 15, 2022).

Industry Training Report. November 2021. https://pubs.royle.com/publication /?m=20617&i=727569&p=24&pp=1&ver=html5 (retrieved March 12, 2022).

Johnstone, K. (1979). *Impro: Improvisation and the Theatre*. New York, NY: Routledge.

Kennedy, R., Dir. 2022. *Downfall: The Case Against Boeing* (film). www.imdb .com/title/tt11893274/ (retrieved March 20, 2022).

Koppett, K. 2012. *Training to Imagine*. Sterling, VA: Stylus.

Lupien, S.J. 2009. "Effects of Stress Throughout the Lifespan on the Brain, Behaviour and Cognition." *Nature Reviews Neuroscience* 10, no. 6, pp. 434–440.

Lupien, S.J., R.P. Juster, C. Raymond, and M. Marin. 2018. "The Effects of Chronic Stress on the Human Brain: From Neurotoxicity, to Vulnerability, to Opportunity." *Frontiers in Neuroendocrinology* 49, pp. 91–105. https://doi .org/10.1016/j.yfrne.2018.02.001 (retrieved March 13, 2022).

Michael, M. 2016. *Where to Invade Next* (film). https://imdb.com/video/vi38854 13401?ref_=vp_rv_ap_0 (retrieved March 19, 2022).

PEW Research. 2021. *Who Doesn't Read Books in America?* www.pewresearch.org /fact-tank/2021/09/21/who-doesnt-read-books-in-america/ (retrieved February 2, 2022).

Press Ganey. October 27, 2021. https://www.pressganey.com/news/press-ganey-study-uncovers-impact-of-diversity-and-equity-on-retention/ (retrieved November 4, 2022).

Psychology Today. October 4, 2021. *The American Workforce Faces Compounding Pressure-Work and Well-Being 2021 Survey Report*. www.apa.org/pubs/reports /work-well-being/compounding-pressure-2021 (retrieved March 19, 2022).

Rogers, E. 2003. *Diffusion of Innovations*, 5th Edition. New York, NY: Free Press.

Schaeffer, M. 2021. *Cumulative Advantage: How to Build Momentum for your Ideas, Business and Life Against All Odds*. Schaeffer Marketing Solutions.

Sinek, S. 2017. *Find Your Why: A Practical Guide for Discovering Purpose for You and Your Team*. New York, NY: Penguin.

Spolin, V. 1963. *Improvisation for the Theatre*. Chicago, IL: Northwestern University Press.

Tedone, A.M. and V. Bruk-Lee 2022. "Speaking Up at Work: Personality's Influence on Employee Voice Behavior." *International Journal of Organizational Analysis* 30, no. 2, pp. 289–304. https://doi.org/10.1108/IJOA-09-2020-2417 (retrieved March 20, 2022).

Tolstory, L. 1943. *What Men Live By, and Other Tales: Annotated*. New York, NY: Pantheon Books.

Tuckman, B.W. 1965. "Developmental Sequence in Small Groups." *Psychological Bulletin* 63, no. 6, pp. 384–99.

# About the Author

**Dr. Candace (Candy) Campbell, DNP, RN, CNL, LNC, CVP, FNAP,** aka: The Innovation Nurse—a transformational keynote speaker, humorist, retreat and workshop leader, award-winning actor, author, and filmmaker. She helps reduce costs of employee turnover and workplace safety issues and increase revenue by facilitating teams to solve communication challenges and make the world a kinder, safer place. Her background in health care spans more than 40 years of clinical, academic, and administrative experience.

As a professional actor and cofounder of an improv company in the early 1990s, she has been gleefully sharing the joys of improv to businesses and people of all ages and stages since 1995. The ability of being able to imagine yourself in someone else's skin (and not taking yourself too seriously) has supported her practice in personal and professional life. For more: https://candycampbell.com

When she's not facilitating improv workshops, executive speech-coaching, or keynoting, she's likely on the road with her third solo show, *An Evening With Florence Nightingale: The Reluctant Celebrity* (https://FlorenceNightingaleLive.com) or playing with her grandkids.

Contact: candy@candycampbell.com for speaking requests or book shipments.

# Index

## OTHER TITLES IN THE HUMAN RESOURCE MANAGEMENT AND ORGANIZATIONAL BEHAVIOR COLLECTION

Michael Provitera, Barry University, Editor

- *Navigating Conflict* by Lynne Curry
- *Innovation Soup* by Sanjay Puligadda and Don Waisanen
- *The Aperture for Modern CEOs* by Sylvana Storey
- *The Future of Human Resources* by Tim Baker
- *Change Fatigue Revisited* by Richard Dool and Tahsin I. Alam
- *Championing the Cause of Leadership* by Ted Meyer
- *Embracing Ambiguity* by Michael Edmondson
- *Breaking the Proactive Paradox* by Tim Baker
- *The Modern Trusted Advisor* by Nancy MacKay and Alan Weiss
- *Achieving Success as a 21st Century Manager* by Dean E. Frost

## Concise and Applied Business Books

The Collection listed above is one of 30 business subject collections that Business Expert Press has grown to make BEP a premiere publisher of print and digital books. Our concise and applied books are for...

- Professionals and Practitioners
- Faculty who adopt our books for courses
- Librarians who know that BEP's Digital Libraries are a unique way to offer students ebooks to download, not restricted with any digital rights management
- Executive Training Course Leaders
- Business Seminar Organizers

Business Expert Press books are for anyone who needs to dig deeper on business ideas, goals, and solutions to everyday problems. Whether one print book, one ebook, or buying a digital library of 110 ebooks, we remain the affordable and smart way to be business smart. For more information, please visit www.businessexpertpress.com, or contact sales@businessexpertpress.com.

www.ingramcontent.com/pod-product-compliance
Lightning Source LLC
Chambersburg PA
CBHW061314220326
41599CB00026B/4880